D0087843

Dave Zobel's
Bent Book *of*
BOATSPEAK

BY

(NOT SURPRISINGLY)
DAVE ZOBEL

WITH RANDOM SCRIBBLINGS BY
JOHN DUSENBERRY

International Marine / McGraw-Hill
Camden, Maine • New York • San Francisco • Washington, D.C. • Auckland
Bogotá • Caracas • Lisbon • London • Madrid • Mexico City • Milan
Montreal • New Delhi • San Juan • Singapore • Sydney • Tokyo • Toronto

International Marine
A Division of The McGraw·Hill Companies

10 9 8 7 6 5 4 3 2 1

Copyright © 2000 Dave Zobel

All rights reserved. The name "International Marine" and the International Marine logo are trademarks of The McGraw-Hill Companies. Printed in the United States of America.

Library of Congress Cataloging-in-Publication Data
Zobel, Dave
    Dave Zobel's bent book of boatspeak / by (not surprisingly) Dave Zobel ; with random scribblings by John Dusenberry.
       p.   cm.
    title: Bent book of boatspeak
    ISBN 0-07-135817-X
    1. Boats and boating—Terminology. 2. Sailing—Terminology. I. Dusenberry, John. II. Title.

GV811 .Z36 2000
797.1'01'4—dc21   00-035089

Contents

*Whom do we appreciate?
Webster! Webster! Hooray!

◆◆◆

Marine Diesel Motors in Brief

Marine Charts in Brief

Marines in Briefs

Strategies for Sailing

Strategies for Rowing

—————————————◆◆◆—————————————

Strategies for Washing Up on the Beach

Part One One More Time

Question and Answer Session

Refreshments

Parting Shots

Acknowledgment

Without

Kinvin,

I would

never

have

learned

most

of what

I've

already

forgotten

about

sailing.

Introduction

Many authors find that the most difficult part of a book to write is the introduction. For it is here that the main subject is supposed to be introduced, in a manner which is engaging without being jarring. Neophyte and veteran writers alike recognize the challenge of launching into a monologue without overwhelming the reader.

Relying on the very latest innovations in computer-aided redaction, the present volume is one of the few published works to circumvent this problem. How does it do this? By saying almost nothing whatsoever about its real subject throughout the entire introduction. Instead, it begins with an unsubstantiated claim (gleaned from the author's own minimal experience and expressed with pompous inexactitude) about what many authors allegedly find difficult. It then goes on to gloat about how it avoids the problem, posing an unnecessary rhetorical question and answering it in a thoroughly incomplete (albeit prolix) manner, including a not at all witty summary of its own structure.

The subject itself does not appear anywhere in the introduction, except in a vague allusion in the last sentence, which waits as long as possible before even mentioning the word SAILING.

◆◆◆

A word on words

As many wise philosophers have noted, a boat is like a dictionary of obsceni-
ties: It's impossible to use to the fullest unless you already know all the
words.

The reason for this, of course, is that without full knowledge of every part
of a boat (or word in a dictionary), you're guaranteed to get lost or end up
spinning in a vicious circle.

For instance, take a completely random but perfectly valid nautical term:
acockbill. (Yes, it's a real word.) What's "acockbill"? We dig out Grandpa's nautical dictionary and find that in reference to something called a *yard,* it means
"not topped horizontally." Fine—but what's a *yard*? Oh, that's something to
which a sail is bent. Then what's *bent*? etc., etc.

If we do this long enough, we are guaranteed to come full circle and end up
precisely where we started from—no better off—not much wiser—but certainly
more exhausted.

Just like sailing.

Yes, nautical terminology is a code—and like any good code,[1] it was
designed primarily to keep outsiders outside. Part of this is due to the fact
that half the words in the code (*scupper, gudgeon, boom,* and the like) seem to
have been made up by a two-year-old (probably the same kid who invented

◆◆◆

1. Not that it *is* a good code. . . .

"googol"), while the other half (*knot*, for example) must have been named by some wily old salt with wobbly dentures and a sense of humor bordering on the perverse.

What's so unusual about *knot*? Nothing at all—except that a *knot* is a unit of speed. The thing that we would call a "knot" (in view of the fact that it connects two pieces of rope together) is actually a *bend*, and the thing we would call a "bend" is actually a *bight*. But *rope* is not the right word either: sailors call it a *sheet*, or sometimes a *shroud* . . . because the thing that *looks* like a big sheet (or a shroud) is called the *main*.[2] And so on.

With boats, therefore, as with dictionaries, you can't really start learning anything until you've learned everything. For instance, say you're hoisting a that-thing-that-somebody-told-you-is-called-a-*gaff*, and much to your discomfiture an eminent colleague takes the opportunity to editorialize, "You fool! She's acockbill!" The only way you'll even know that the guy is talking to you (assuming your name's not Bill), let alone what he's talking about, is if you're already such an expert at sailing that you'd never be so foolish as to commit the gaffe of hoisting a gaff acockbill in the first place. Non-experts will quickly find themselves stymied.

Until now, that is. Take this slim and elegant volume in hand, study carefully, and be amazed at the confidence in your own voice as you hear your-

---

2. Then again, the *stern sheets* are an area in a rowboat containing neither sheets, nor ropes, nor much of anything else, really. This is why rowboats are no longer used for mail delivery: because of the Postal Service's dictum regarding "neither main, nor row, nor sheet, nor boom of bight. . . ."

self hollering back at your interlocutor that yes, she's acockbill, but at least she's not upside-down.[3]

(For your reference: If someone does suddenly opine, "She's acockbill!" and you have no idea what that means, the proper face-saving response is: "Sure is!" or perhaps: "And don't you just love her for it!" or even, blushing modestly: "Gosh! Thanks!")

You are on the path of wisdom. By purchasing this high-quality reference book (and such a slim one! and so elegant!), you have taken the first important step toward understanding the secret language of sailing. Congratulate yourself. (You can be sure the publisher is congratulating *himself*.)

And now, prepare to open your mind to a whole new way of speaking— not just about acockbill yards, but about everything maritime, acockbill or not. Indeed, in less time than it takes to say, "Shut up about acockbill already!" you will find yourself well on the way to becoming a slim (to say nothing of elegant) master sailor. You can finally converse with slim old salts and . . . er . . . elegant longshoremen, with astonishing fluency.

Provided they spend the majority of their time discussing yards getting hoisted all acockbill.

Keep your ears open—it might happen.

3. But don't try to hoist a gaff or a yard (or an interlocutor) with this (or any) slim and elegant volume in hand. Better to hoist with both hands free. If nothing else, this will at least make it less likely that the thing will come up all acockbill.

    And rest assured that whether or not you read any further, you'll never forget what "acockbill" means—just from seeing it so many times on this slim (and elegant) page.

A word on gender

Perhaps surprisingly (for biology majors, anyway), every water vessel—ocean liner, submarine, or pair of soggy twigs bound together with twine—is a lady. Or at least claims to be. Like that strange neighbor you used to have.

Regardless of how they look in fishnets, boats and their constituent parts are traditionally referred to as "she," for reasons which are shrouded in the m(isogyn)ists of time. (Admiral Nimitz used to claim that it was because it costs so much to keep one in paint and powder. Mrs. Nimitz used to give him a black eye for that, every time.)

Boat captains and crewmembers are traditionally referred to as "he," for the reason that the comments most often applied to them refer to canine lines of descent terminating in a male.

Because of the potential for pronoun confusion and misconstrued sexism, which often leads to letter writings and book burnings,[4] this book will refer to everything on a boat (including the crew) as "it," but not consistently, for the reason that we jolly well feel like her, and if y'all don't agree with our, that's just too bad for theirselfs.

---

4. Buy 'em! Burn 'em! We'll just print more.

no·men·cla·ture—*n* : the naming of parts. From the Latin words *nomen* (= "the naming") + *clature* (= "pretending to know Latin").

Let's get STARTED!

or

Faking CAN *only* get you so FAR

In Shakespeare's first draft of *The Merchant of Venice*, a minor character named Polio, out on a jaywalking tour of Venice, pauses to wring out his clothes and is immediately accosted by one Drānio, intent on selling him a boat before the real owner shows up. Polio's suspicions are aroused, however, by the fact that Drānio obviously doesn't know the first thing about boats.

What tips him off? The words Drānio uses to refer to various parts of the boat. For instance, the object which any Elizabethan old salt worth his old salt would never call anything but "Yon skean wherefrom an harl doth fain prevail / To wend his course withal unto the sail" (now abbreviated to "a cleat") Drānio calls "That kind o' shiny thingummy o'er there." Polio's disclosure of this crucial fact to the cops, and the thrilling high-speed gondola chase that follows, might never have happened if only Drānio had had at his disposal (or anywhere else in his kitchen) a working knowledge of the boating jargon.

But no one can become an expert overnight. Anyone acquiring a new vocabulary must always pass through the Three Stages of Faking:

1. The Indicative Stage

Characterized by frantic pointing and the frequent appearance of the phrase "that thing over there."

ANDREA: Storm's comin' in. Quick, grab that thing over there.

DORIA: Gotcha.

ANDREA: Eh? No, no. *That* thing. Not *that* thing. *That* thing. Over *there*.

DORIA: This thing? Here? Or this other thing, . . . over here?

ANDREA: (*exasperated*) *That* thing! Over THERE!

DORIA: Oh, *this* thing! And do what with it?

ANDREA: Umm . . . just leave it there.

2. The A Little Knowledge Is a Dangerous Thing Stage

The sophomore has learned a few words ("yar," "thar she blows," "you fool") and now slings them around on every possible occasion as if he knew what they really meant:

LUCY: Cap'n—it's a hurricane! What'll we do?

TANIA: (*consulting manual*) Uh . . . "Steady As She Goes"?

LUCY: But the helm's not responding! We're foundering!

TANIA:	(*consulting manual again*) Er . . . "Steady *AS* She Goes"?
LUCY:	We're sinking fast! We have to abandon ship!
TANIA:	(*gaining confidence*) . . . "Steady As *SHE* Goes"!
LUCY:	But blub blub glub blubblub. . . .
TANIA:	"Blebby Blabbee *GLOEB*! . . ."

3. The Inscrutable Stage

At this stage, our colloquists completely eschew their normal vocabularies in favor of words far more obscure than "colloquists" and "eschew," and only a fellow Inscrutable can make any sense of what is being said (which, after all, is the whole idea):

QUEEG:	(*with menace*) Pay out ye binnacle abaft her topsides—
QUEEQUEG:	(*frowning*) Nah, scupper by the forward nor'easter line on a beam reach.
QUEEG:	(*confused*) . . . And thwart me windage with bulkheads aweigh?
QUEEQUEG:	(*smugly*) Ha! Not without scullin' a fantail!
QUEEG:	(*giggling*) I love it when you talk dirty.

If you are in the first stage of development, where everything is still "that thing over there," just remember that it is possible to go from being thought of as a complete idiot to being thought of as a partial idiot simply by inserting one of the following words before every utterance of the word "thing":

HARD   taɴɢly

soft   wʀɪɴᴋʟʏ

soggy   ɪᴄᴋʏ

ᴅʀʏ   *invisible*

unfriendly   *magical*

Fɪɢ. 118.—Environmental Hazards; №. 63: *Dry rot.* (From an engraving by Müschnijck.)

Most things on a boat fit into one of these ten categories ("that hard thing over there," "that soggy thing you just sat on," "that wrinkly thing coming on board—oh—hi, honey," etc.). Anything that doesn't is probably not important and can be jettisoned at a convenient time (preferably when nobody's watching).

◆◆◆

HARD *things*

I must down to the seas again,
to the lonely sea and the sky,
And all I ask is a tall blonde,
and a bar with beer nearby.
—Jayne Masefield, *Seafood Mama*

For most people, sailing is all about avoiding injury, and the most enjoyable outings are those which do not include a trip to the emergency room (or—worse—a burial at sea). The most dangerous things you will encounter (besides insane captains, sharks who believe their own PR, et al.) are usually the hard things, so if nothing else, you ought to learn their names and locations. This way, you can avoid diving into them headfirst, skewering other people with them, attempting to eat them, etc.

The following discussion separates the hard things by size. Larger sizes represent better values.

Quite enormously BIG hard things

The biggest hard thing in the vicinity of the boat *is* the boat. There are several basic types of boats (all hard), from barrels to floating cities. Each is distinguished from the others in ways which make little or no sense but which must still be learned in order to avoid the sort of physical injury which generally results from gravely offending a boat owner.

The most obvious distinction is between **boat**—meaning "puny little tub" (as in: "Have you got any room for my in-laws on your boat?"), and **ship**—meaning "majestic watercraft" (as in: "Heck, you could drive a *tank* onto my ship—but let's see your in-laws").

Terms mainly useful for impressing innocent bystanders include *sloop*, *smack*, **star**, SHELL, skiff, scull, *scow*, **dhow**, HOY, barge, VESSEL, launch, gig, shallop, ketch, *yawl*, yacht, RAFT, craft, **hovercraft**, PERSONAL WATERCRAFT,[5] punt, **JUNK**,[6] J/24, buss, sailfish, SUNFISH, *dugout*, FRIGATE, ferry, wherry, dandy, *dory*, **SHARPIE**, garvey, galley, GALLEON, galleass, gondola, **dragon**, DREADNOUGHT, pinnace, *PIROGUE*, **PROA**, *pram*, peapod, KAYAK, umiak, saic, jangada, ***canoe***, CORVETTE,[7] corsair, caravel, coracle, COCKLESHELL, cog, coble, caïque, carack, **catamaran**, *trimaran,* sampan, RANDAN, *merchantman*, man-o'-war, WISHBONE, thalamegus, lorcha,

5. So much nicer than the impersonal ones of earlier times.
6. In former times restricted to Chinese waters, but now to be found floating in every harbor of the world.
7. Not a very practical vehicle, but great for picking up chicks—except that there's no back seat to speak of.

◆◆◆

aphractus, argosy, baggala, felucca, ***tartane***, wanigan, *ULTRALIGHT*, LATEEN,[8] ʙɪʀᴇᴍᴇ, **TRIREME**, *quadrireme*, ᴅᴀʜᴀʙᴇᴀʜ, and ***XEBEC***.

Others are ʀᴏᴡʙᴏᴀᴛ, showboat, lifeboat, *flyboat*, **bumboat**, ꜰʟᴀᴛʙᴏᴀᴛ, *tugboat*, ꜱᴛᴇᴀᴍʙᴏᴀᴛ, ʀɪᴠᴇʀʙᴏᴀᴛ, longboat, ***catboat***, ʜᴏᴜꜱᴇʙᴏᴀᴛ, **cockboat**, iceboat, ᴜ-ʙᴏᴀᴛ, *PT boat*, **canal boat**, and ᴛᴜɴᴀ ʙᴏᴀᴛ, as well as *scooter*, ꜱᴄʜᴏᴏɴᴇʀ, **clipper**, cutter, *GUNTER*, coaster, ᴛᴇɴᴅᴇʀ, trawler, **troller**, *whaler*, ***trailer/sailer***, tanker, ʜᴏᴏᴋᴇʀ, bilander, collier, *lighter*, ʟɪɴᴇʀ, **STEAMER**, *lateener*,[9] ***dredger***, crabber, freighter, dogger, ʟᴜɢɢᴇʀ, **jigger**, outrigger, ꜱQᴜᴀʀᴇ-ʀɪɢɢᴇʀ, sandbagger, *windsurfer*, ᴍɪɴᴇꜱᴡᴇᴇᴘᴇʀ, ***purse seiner***, ᴅᴇꜱᴛʀᴏʏᴇʀ, **submarine**, cruiser, **battleship**, and *CARRIER* (at five pegs, the hardest to sink).

More precise terms include **brig**, which refers to absolutely any boat whatsoever (as long as it has two square-rigged masts, a quadrilateral gaff sail abaft the mizzenmast, and at least two headsails), and **bark** (or **barque**[10]), a generic term which also means any boat whatsoever (but most particularly those which have all their masts square-rigged except the mizzenmast, which is fore-and-aft rigged). Memorize this, bearing in mind that newcomers to the

---

8. All that romaines of the Romaine Empire.
9. Like a lateen, only lateenier.
10. Which you can stop pronouncing somewhere near the middle. Do not be distressed by the presence of so many silent letters in a word. Virtually any unfamiliar nautical term can be pronounced correctly if you simply growl enough. Anyway, *barque* is worse than *bight*.

colorful world of sailing are sometimes confused by the unrelated word **brig**, which is an on-board prison (as if that weren't redundant).

Other types of boats include **brigantine** (which is like a **brig**, only more so) and **barkentine** (which is like a bark, only less so). In some of the swankier European ports, you may also encounter a **hermaphrodite brig**[11] trying to pick up a mooring by making repeated passes at it.

Some boats have boats of their own. Many yachts proudly sport a **dinghy**, a little toy boat whose main function is to maneuver back and forth in crowded harbors while its oars make small dents (or "d'oar dinghs") in other people's shiny new **cabin cruisers**.[12]

The following mnemonic should help you instantly determine the type of any given boat:

Ask The Owner.

(Be sure to nod knowingly at his response, to indicate that that's what you were thinking all along.)

♦♦♦

11. The original something-for-everyone design. Smile and make polite conversation, but do not attempt to follow it home.
12. Note the insertion of the silent "h" to distinguish *dinghy* from the adjective which best describes it. For centuries researchers have labored to uncover a suitable euphemism for *dinghy*, without success. (Jocular optimists have tried to palm off terms like **jolly boat** on the rest of us, but they aren't fooling anyone.)

BIG **HARD** things

Nothing on a boat is as big and hard and nasty as the boat itself—but many things come close.

Big hard nasty things to watch out for include **bulkheads**, which are the filthy things that pass for walls; **overheads**, which are the filthy things that pass for ceilings; and **decks**, which are the filthy things that pass for floors (and which are generally scattered with **deck chairs**, which are the filthy things that pass for chairs). The **bulwarks** is (or are) not a bulkhead; it (or them) is (or am) a special wall around the deck which restricts the passengers' access to the ocean but not vice versa.

Bulkheads and overheads are not the only heads you will encounter. Heads abound on ships—and what can be a merrier sight than a ship full of abounding heads? The area underneath the deck is the **deckhead**, where quite a collection of interesting flora may be found. The object resembling a stovepipe and blowing smoke up your behind is the **smoke head**—or possibly the first mate. There are also the heads of fellow crewmembers—hard objects in their own right, for the most part, often to be found sharing gossip around the **scuttlebutt** (office water cooler)—not to mention the **head** itself, which is the toilet, and into which we will venture no further (and we recommend that you do likewise).

Use caution when shouting out words like *deckhead* and *scuttlebutt*, lest seamen with sensitive egos take it personally.

SMALL FAT **HARD** things

There are many causes of bruises on cruises. Big hard things are the usual suspects, but plenty of smaller objects also enjoy inflicting serious bodily harm. Some of them may not even be attached to the boat (particularly after a few minutes of rough sailing).

Bitts and **bollards** are posts for securing lines to, using any of a variety of knots which a sailor wishes he had paid more attention to learning back in Cub Scouts. The only difference between a bitt and a bollard is whether it is mounted on a boat (a bitt) or not (a bollard).[13] Interestingly, the expression

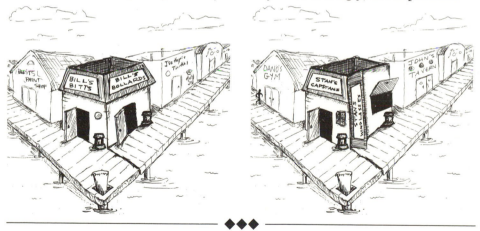

13. A bollard looks like a bitt stuck on a dock, a bitt looks like a **capstan** stuck in neutral, and a capstan looks like a **windlass** stuck on sideways, if that's of any use to you.

◆◆◆

"to the bitter end" derives from the **bitter end** of an anchor line, which is whichever end was supposed to have been tied to something (viz., a bitt—or actually, viz a goot shtrong knot). The "-er" ending refers to the fact that this end is "bitter" (= more bitt) than the other end. (This is true even if this end is only a little itty-bitty bit bitter than the other end.) The other end is supposed to be tied to the anchor and is, naturally, ancher than this end.

A **buoy** is a floating anchored channel marker; the shoddily constructed ones tend not to work well, but every good buoy does fine. Buoys are colored (red, green, or black) and numbered (even or odd)—just like the slots on a roulette wheel.[14] The names for the various types of buoys are terribly clever. A **can** looks for all the world like a can that is darkish and roundish, and hence rather boulderish at a distance of thirty feet or more. On closer inspection, however (i.e., just before impact), a can can be seen to have an odd number painted on it. A **nun**, on the other hand, is conical and red and has an *even* number painted on it, which is easy to remember because it looks[15] like a nun who . . . er . . . is conical and red and has an even number painted on her.

Binnacles and **barnacles**—one of which is a compass case and the other of which is not a compass case, but honestly, who can say which is which?—are particularly hard round objects, designed to withstand a

◆◆◆

14. This is not the only way in which sailing resembles roulette.
15. Uncannily.

direct physical assault. Direct physical assaults (at least on compass cases) are usually due to frustrated helmsmen (the more frustrated the helmsman, the more direct the assault) and are a common method of proving that there's at least one thing on this earth that the helmsman can still find.

Barnacles are nasty and sharp (thus distinguishing themselves from most of the people you will encounter on the high seas, who tend not to be so sharp). En masse, they have a texture approximating that of a barbed-wire scouring pad, which accounts for the staggering popularity of **keelhauling**, a maritime hazing ritual in which the ~~victim~~ new pledge is tied up and dragged underwater along the entire length of the barnacle-encrusted keel. The results are more or less predictable . . . and the barnacles don't like it much, either.[16]

Despite its name (and its brief appearance in the X-rated version of *Peter Pan*), the **breasthook** is neither a breast nor a hook, but merely a structure at the nose of a small boat which allows the entire boat to be slung over the shoulder and carried like an overcoat. It is included in this section only because it too begins with the letter B.

---

16. Ref.: Dale Barnacly, *How to Skin Friends and Influence People.*

◆◆◆

LONG POINTY **HARD** things

Mothers tend to fear ships because of the prevalence of long, narrow objects with sharp ends, with which a great deal of fun can be had until someone's eye gets put out (and then all the sorrys in the world won't bring it back). Pointy objects include masts, yards, and assorted sticks and hooks.

Everyone knows what a **mast** is,[17] but none but the most hideously naïve would assume that a boat can only have one. Some boats have one; some have more than one; many start out with more than one and gradually (or rapidly) dwindle to zero. And lo, unto every mast a name has been given. The **Foremast** is foremost. The **maInmast** (exact derivation of name unknown) is the main mast; it is usually the strongest mast and is therefore the best one to be lashed to when approaching Sirens. The **mizzenmasT**, apparently an afterthought, definitely an after *mast*, iz often mizzen on zmall boatz.

The largest schooner ever built (outside of the prairie) had *seven* masts, named Spanker, Driver, Jigger, Frigger, Sleepy, Bashful, and Dock. (Reports of a cruise director with skin white as snow have not been confirmed.)

At the top of a mast is a pointy bit dubbed the . Scholars have long argued that since this is, after all, the mast top, it ought to have been given the name "masttop"; but it wasn't, and the reason for this is known only to the dub who dubbed it. This intentional reversal of words for no good reason what-

◆◆◆

17. A pointy object with one end stuck in the deck. You already knew that.

soever (also evident in *topsides*—the tops of the sides) rages many people out and just serves as a reminder of what obstinate headbutts sailors can be.

The best-known spar (after the mast[18]) is the **boom,** a massive, heavy bar which swings around wildly near head level. The large number of near misses between sailors' heads and the boom led to the invention of the **boom vang,** a piece of tightly stretched cord designed to keep the boom exactly *at* head level. The boom and the other movable spars, large and small, are especially user-inimical when, with the assistance of a mischievous wind, they **sky** (= point straight up in the air), often as a way of stalling for time while deciding whose head would be the most fun to glance off of.

18. Or, in one well-publicized case, a full two years before it.

◆◆◆

The larger and more dangerous end of a spar is usually the **butt end** (by analogy with the corresponding end of a sailor), but the pointy end can be dangerous, too. For example, the **bowsprit**, which sticks off the pointy end of the boat, has a pointy end of its own which is useful for impaling other boats. Sticking off the other end of the boat is the **bumpkin**, which is actually just a bowsprit onto which the wrong end of a boat has been glued. (Some people call the bumpkin the **boomkin**, as in: "Anything boomkin do bumpkin do better; I kin do anything better than yawl.")

—— ❖❖❖ ——

SOFT *things*

The Owl and the Pussycat went to sea
In a beautiful pea-green boat—
"Great view! Great food!" the Pussy mewed.
"But these feathers sure stick in your throat."
—Edward Bear,
Enjoy Life—Eat Out More Often

The simple fact is that there are very few things on or near a boat that are in any way soft to begin with.

The only one worth discussing is the **fender**, which is a device sticking out from the sides of a boat to allow it to crash willy-nilly into others sideways. (There is a correspondingly named device on cars, used for the identical purpose.)

It would be amusingly optimistic to search for **bunk**, or **cushion**, or **waterlogged clothes that have been drying in the sun and wind** in this chapter.

Do not be misled by activities suggesting the presence (or recent departure) of softness. For instance, pointing the boat juuust a little more into the wind is given the uproariously clever name of **hardening up**. In reality, nothing hardens. Everything is already hard.

Angst

By now, it should be apparent to the careful reader (if he's out there) that this whole business may be tougher than first imagined. Many parts of a boat have been given non-intuitive names; some have been given names without really deserving one at all.

At this point, therefore, it might help to note that many of the remaining terms in this book are sensible and obvious.

It might help—but it would be a lie.

Consider the issue of false plurals. *Topsides* does not mean "more than one topside." *The bends* is not what you get when you have more than one bend. *Lines, ways, waters, stays, sheets*: all of these mean something other than "a line [or a way, or a water, or a stay, or a sheet] . . . and another one, too." But this does not mean that words ending in *-s* are *never* plural. And some words appearing to be singular actually aren't; for instance, on a chart, a compass rose actually consists of *two* roses (one outer and one inner), meaning that a rose is a rose in a rose.[19] Finally, note that some words, like *athwartships* and *bows*, mean the same thing with *or without* the -s, and are therefore their own plural (or plurals) (or pluralses).

Likewise, it is risky to extrapolate from Nature. A sail has a head, but

19. First noticed by G. Stein.

it has no tail; a block, on the other hand, has a tail, but it has no head.[20] Plenty of other body parts can be found on boats (including the sole, the heel, the foot, the leg, the knee, the backbone, the rib, the shoulder, the eye, nose, and throat—even the buttock line, thank you very much), but generally not in their customary locations.

The quantity of animals immortalized in the argot also boggles the mind: horses, hounds, bulldogs, rats, cats, dogs, mice, geese, sheep, crows, pelicans, dolphins, turtles, monkeys—all can be found lurking among the parts of a ship, in name if not in actual physical form.

Nor is this a realm of human endeavor in which precision counts but little—to coin a pompous phrase. When the skipper suggests, two inches (= 5 cm) from your ear, that a prudent sailor in your situation would doubtless consider the very near future an appropriate juncture at which to hoist a *pennant,* it would be unwise to assume that hoisting a *pendant* would make him just as happy. And of course, who among us has not committed the amusing error of *reeving,* when what was requested was *reefing?*[21]

The deep blue sea is full of hilarious tales of instances in which nautical terms were misheard or misunderstood by well-intentioned sailors.

The deep blue sea is also full of well-intentioned sailors.

Study carefully.

20. Except for the blockhead at the helm.
21. Hands down, please; it was a rhetorical question.

CAP'N SEAMUS'S HANDY HINTS #1065: *In an emergency, your spinnaker can perform double duty as a sea anchor. (Discoverer unknown.)*

SOGGY *things*

Water, water, everywhere,
Nor any drop to drink:
What was *your rush?! I said don't flush!—*
The sump pump's on the blink.
—Salmon Tater Coleslaw,
For This *I Missed the Garter Toss?!*

Water is your friend, they say,[22] but in reality, this is true only to the extent that it would be still more impossible to sail your boat than it already is if there weren't something wet to float it on. Unfortunately water, like an annoying roommate, has a habit of hanging around and going through all your stuff despite your having specifically asked it not to. Therefore, most of the things you'll observe on a boat (or in a mirror on a boat) will be in some stage of dampness.

You're soaking in it

Sailing would be difficult enough if the surface across which the vehicle

22. Ref.: Ernestine and Horatio W. They, Jr., *Collected Sayings. Vol. VI:* Amity *to* Aqueous.

◆◆◆

moves were solid, flat, and at rest (the way a linoleum skating rink is). However, centuries of careful observation have revealed water to be liquid, wobbly, and rarely motionless—a meteorological condition which the scientific community has designated **waves**.

Waves in excess around a boat can cause it to do some rather exciting things. Waves in excess inside a boat can redefine the word "exciting." Most of the challenges in sailing can be blamed on the perpetual disagreement between environment, vehicle, and operator regarding which of them is to be master. Boats spend most of their time trying to gain mastery over waves; sailors spend most of their time trying to gain mastery over boats; and waves spend most of their time trying to gain mastery over sailors. It's like an enormous game of Rock, Paper, Scissors.

GLOSSARY

self-draining cockpit—
That area of a boat which most faithfully duplicates all the sensations of crouching in a constantly flushing toilet.

The first inkling you may have that the sea is considering making a claim on your person is an increase in the **swell** (that is, the waves). Always be polite and wave back, to show what a swell time you wish you were having. As the swell approaches a predefined threshold (e.g., the height of the mainmast), the crew may begin submitting informal requests for supernatural intercession. Incantations of this sort often begin with a shriek and end with a splutter.

Weather permitting, the ship may become relatively humid at this moment, via a process known as **shipping water**. Bailing is recommended. A boat almost as damp on the inside as on the outside is said to be **swamped**. This is an indication that something is wrong.

" . . . *rarely will [bailing] prove efficacious absent prior ascertainment of*
. . . *the principal source of the influx of seawater.*"
—*Practically Seamanship*, 1802 ed., pp. 411 ff.

◆◆◆

But the fun is not over yet. The boat will keep trying to swallow the ocean (and vice versa), until at some point, the entire body of water effectively gains access to every part of the craft (and the crew). Now is a good time for those on board to think seriously about alternative transport.

Some boats show a distinct talent for filling with water. Rather than going to all the trouble of gradually admitting a trickle here, a dribble there, they simply and haughtily flop themselves over sideways at the first drop of spray, in a Shakespearian act of self-destruction referred to (inexplicably) as **capsizing**. Capsizing may be viewed as evidence of carelessness or unsea-worthiness; nevertheless, it is an effective way to make a direct impression on the crews of nearby watercraft (particularly if they are closer than the height of the mast).

Truly artistic boats, not satisfied with the indeterminacy of capsizing, actually go completely upside-down in one fell swoop. The technical term for this activity is **turning ʇnɹʇɟǝ**; the word *turtle* refers to the resulting shape and speed of the boat—and perhaps to the intelligence of the skipper as well. The paradox of turning turtle is that although it restores the mast to a vertical orientation and lowers wind resistance to almost zero, the speed of the boat actually *decreases.* Scientists have long sought to understand the reason for this phenomenon; although the solution remains elusive, there is still every reason to hope for a breakthrough.

◆◆◆

TOO *much* of a good thing

Ever since the days of Prince Henry the Navigator (whose maps of African waterways are rivaled only by those of his younger brother, Prince Albert the Alligator), sailors have recognized that knowing where you are is almost as important as having a general idea of where you thought you might like to go. The problem is that, as Prince Henry himself concluded after decades of detailed scrutiny, most of the ocean looks like most of the rest of the ocean. This is why maps generally show the ocean as a big flat featureless blob. (The word "ocean" itself is thought to derive from an ancient language, intermediate between Greek and Egyptian—the so-called "Helle-Coptic"—and may be related to a root meaning "that big flat featureless blob o' mine.")

There are, of course, plenty of terms for pieces of water where land is visible nearby. Channels, sounds, lagoons; firths, fords, fjords; bights, basins, bays, bayous; deltas, marinas, inlets, outlets, estuaries, tributaries; waterways, seaways, fairways, euripi, narrow straits, straight narrows, harbors, havens, rivers, coves, and gulves—all are easy to name (if not to distinguish) by glancing at the shape of the land around them. The challenge is to be able to know where you are when you are far away from land, where there is no actual visible difference between *this* vast patch of water over *here* and *that* one over *there.*

Traditionally, one of the best-trusted methods of navigation has been **sounding**—that is, measuring the distance to the ocean floor, comparing it to

◆◆◆

some number on some chart, and making a sound of dismay. **Celestial navigation** is another method; this involves invoking a celestial being while scanning the heavens for familiar constellations (and making a sound of dismay). The question is what to do when the water is too deep for sounding, the stars aren't shining, or you have laryngitis. The answer, if there is one, has still not been found (or perhaps it has been found but was then lost at sea).

One approach espoused by some (married) people has been to make use of man-made landmarks. Alas, most attempts at fixing landmarks in the ocean, from building rock piles to painting a big **✗** on the side of the boat, have tended to be resounding failures (which is to say, they tended to be sounding failures the first time around).

Another important discovery made in the early days of sailing was that none of the conventions of land-based traffic control were well suited to aquatic use. STOP signs tended to sink, painted lane markings refused to hold their shape, and orange highway cones had an annoying habit of drifting up to the sixtieth parallel and clustering there.

Until a solution is discovered, international convention will continue to use the phrase "the open ocean" to refer to the wide-open parts of the ocean: those parts that aren't near anywhere interesting (what a car driver would call "the open road," if it were a road, and he were particularly interested in discussing it).

[Note: Effective Saturday, the open ocean will be closed until further notice.]

◆◆◆

Splish, splash, glug, glug
(or Glug, glug, splish, splash)

Owing to the confusion surrounding the large number of liquids available on or near the sea, as well as the multiple interpretations of the term "a tight ship," we will now attempt to explain both of the meanings of the word **drink**.

A drink is the wet thing that ends up in many a drunken sailor.

The drink is the wet thing that many a drunken sailor ends up in.

DRY *things*

USAGE QUIZ #1

Test your knowledge of nautical terminology by taking the following quiz. Do not reveal your responses to anyone. Entries remain the property of the publisher. The decision of the judges is final. All rights reserved. Patent pending. Litho in the U.S.A. A pint's a pound the world around.

1. Select the least inaccurate translation of the following sentence: "Shiver me timbers, matey, for ye be a swabby landlubber!"
   - ☐ a. "I am surprised, nautical associate, to learn that you are a lower-echelon mop-wielding person who dislikes ocean travel!"
   - ☐ b. "Vibrate my structural supports, O life partner, since you shun the pelagic and use cotton-tipped sticks for cosmetic purposes!"
   - ☐ c. "Hey, buddy—I've merely flipped this book open and memorized a few random words!"
   - ☐ d. "Welcome to the Pirates of the Caribbean ride!"

2. Which of the following has the highest resale value?
   - ☐ a. One pound of flotsam.
   - ☐ b. Two kilos of jetsam.
   - ☐ c. Three gallons of bilge water.
   - ☐ d. All the empty beer cans at the bottom of Boston Harbor.

3. Take the following out of chronological order:

    ___a. sailing

    ___b. bailing

    ___c. flailing

    ___d. impaling

4. Under what circumstances would you yourself be inclined to swear like a sailor?
    How so?_____

5. Which is the best way to avoid running aground in unfamiliar waters?

    ☐   a. Consult all available navigational charts, take frequent soundings, keep in
        constant VHF contact with the USCG, and post extra lookouts.

    ☐   b. Install modern sonar and GPS equipment, download the latest updates to
        the ship's navigational software, and lower an independently maneuver-
        able remotely operated submersible on a two-kilometer tether.

    ☐   c. Charter a fleet of nuclear submarines to travel in phalanx formation ahead
        of your Sailfish, sending back constant reports.

    ☐   d. Get no closer to the sea than this book.

6. Rewrite the first chapter of *20,000 Leagues Under the Sea,* paying particular atten-
    tion to the baseball franchise expansion possibilities._____

7. If the wind's in your starboard quarter, and you're sailing by the lee, and the chute's aluff, and the thwart's awash, and the beer's a-gone, you should:
    - ☐ a. Grab this sailing book.
    - ☐ b. Grab a *proper* sailing book.
    - ☐ c. Grab anything.
    - ☐ d. Abandon ship.

8. On first boarding an unfamiliar ship, it is a matter of strictest seaman's etiquette to take pains to familiarize oneself with all the equipment found thereon so that when the time comes, it will be possible to:
    - ☐ a. Assist the skipper in bailing.
    - ☐ b. Point out features that any decent boat ought to have, although this one doesn't appear to.
    - ☐ c. Find the shortest route to the storage locker containing the beer.
    - ☐ d. Abandon ship.

9. Plot a course between any of the following. Subtract one point for each statute mile traveled overland.
    - a. Salina to Salinas (or Karachi to Caracas).
    - b. Montpelier (or Montpellier) to Monterey (or Monterrey).
    - c. Encinitas to Ensenada (returning via Grenada and Granada).
    - d. Dneprodzerzhinsk to Székesfehérvár.

10. Confess: You did think *xebec* was some kind of Tibetan wildebeest, didn't you?

 ☐ yes   ☐ sure

11. Cite at least two medieval references showing that it is at least hypothetically possible for a sailor man of medium build to live in a garbage can.

1._____

2._____

UNFRIENDLY *things*

Bobby Shaftoe's gone to sea,
Silver buckles on his knee,
Buff and tough . . . er. . . like . . . er . . . Kenny Gee-ee . . . ?
Pret-ty Bobby Shaaafff-tooooe.
—M. Goose,
Bobby Shaaafff-tooooe

Of all the dangerous things on a vessel, many of which can cause you grave bodily harm when you stumble upon them unexpectedly, the most dangerous by far are the living ones—the ones who can follow you as you retreat to a safe place and cause you grave bodily harm there as well.

Newcomers to the maritime world are often astonished at the large number of antipathetic peripatetics they encounter on board. Even the friendly ones are usually unbearably ugly.

For safety's sake, contemporary nautical wisdom now holds that it is best to avoid everyone everywhere, insofar as is possible. This flies directly in the face of humanity's need to socialize, which is a pity, since (let's face it) you can never rub elbows with too many **swabbies**, **gobs**, **tars**, **mangees**, and **sea dogs**. (True, these words may seem more at home in an infectious diseases ward than in polite company; yet they still manage to convey a certain ineffable charm, due to their undeniable *je-ne-sais-rien*.)

The shortage of romance on the high seas

It is a common mistake, although a costly one, to misinterpret the level of affection between crewmembers. Do not assume that just because someone hails you with such endearing epithets as "me hearty" or "laddie boy" or "ye lily-livered varmint," he is in any way passing favorable judgment upon your enthusiasm, your youthfulness, or the condition of your internal organs. Such modes of address, in fact, have nothing whatever to do with how the speaker feels about the speakee, and in many cases, the most accurate translation of each of these speech patterns would be "you moron." Sailors just are not that attracted to one another. When you get right down to it, the **bosun's mate** is really only a good friend of the bosun.

And what is a **bosun**, when he's at home? A **boatswain**,[23] of course. But not just anyone can be a boatswain; swaining—especially swaining a boat— is a difficult and dangerous job best left to the professionals. Do not confuse the boatswain with the **coxswain**—pronounced "cocks-'n' " (as in

---

23. I.e., a male admirer (swain) of a boat (boat). In the Moist Olympic Games of 1813, *boatswain* edged out *forecastle* and *topgallant* by a narrow margin to win the coveted Largest Number of Unused Letters (in a Drama or Miniseries) award.

"cocks 'n' bulls") and *never* any other way (some things do not need to be swained nearly so frequently as boats do). Such a large number of people stumble over the pronunciation of "coxswain" that the word is now primarily used as a shibboleth to weed out landlubbers, novices, and other evil pretenders.

GLOSSARY

bumpkin—*The captain, before they put a uniform on him.*

SIR yes SIR

Every ancient navy of the world, like any self-respecting boys' club, organized its members in a strict hierarchy (or pecking order). Emily Post addresses at length the subtle rules and nuances of this complicated, venerated system, but in general, the number of stripes on a uniform sleeve serves as a reasonably accurate indicator of how fully you should take the wearer's suggestions to heart. Nobody thinks much of ignoring a **midshipman** (so-called because he is usually found doubled over amidships, his face the color of algae), but it is a rare sailor who feels comfortable addressing the **admiral** as "Hey, you!" (given that the more correct form of address would be "Hey, you admiral!").

One person you must on no account fail to heed is the **skipper**, an incompetent whose main talent lies in yelling absurd and contradictory orders to other incompetents, whose main talent lies in ignoring anything yelled at them. No, it's often not the skipper's own boat, and no, he doesn't necessarily have any better an idea of where it's heading than anyone else does, but he *is* the one in charge of getting you there and telling you how you're going to help him do it (notwithstanding his frequent allusions to an intrinsically warmer destination). If you ignore him, there's no telling where you could end up, whereas if you listen to him carefully and obey his every command, there's no telling where you could end up.

Speed bump.

◆◆◆

Oddly, however, the most important people on the boat are the ones at the bottom of the totem pole: the **hands**. The responsibility (but not necessarily actual tendency) of these tireless, cheerful ambassadors of nautical good humor is to perform useful labor on a ship. At other times they serve mainly as movable ballast. You can often get away with ignoring orders shouted at you by officers, but it is almost always fatal to ignore a threat muttered by a hand behind his hand.

◆◆◆

PLACES *not* TO GO

The boy stood on the burning deck,
Charred matches strewn around him:
Ashamed to wake his Pa, by heck—
That's where Forensics found him.
                                    —Felicia He-Man,
                                    Now *We're Cookin'!*

A ship is like a home—a home with an extremely large swimming pool in the backyard. And just as a house has a cellar, an attic, a corner of the garage stacked high with old newspapers, etc.—a boat doesn't. Besides this, the main difference between a ship and a home is that mail delivery is slightly more predictable on a ship.

As to the three most important aspects of homeownership (namely, location, location, and location): if you don't like your boat's location,[24] you can always weigh anchor and take your home-away-from-home away from home. But beware: there are many locations *within* your floating home where you

◆◆◆

24. Or location, or location.

will be not merely unwelcome but downright in the way. It is important to learn the names and locations of these locations so that having been thrown out of one, you will not immediately get yourself thrown out of another.

Where not to go

The most important place where you will never be welcome is the **helm**. The helm can be thought of as the driver's seat plus the vast expanse of space (sometimes as many as four cubic inches) around it. It contains one very irritated helmsman. Stay away. You cannot make him less irritated.

On large boats, the helm is found in a stuffy room called the **bridge**,[25] where the helmsman is encouraged to stand in monotonous discomfort. On small boats, the helm is found in a watery pit called the **cockpit**, where the helmsman is permitted to sit in a puddle of ice water. The worst features of both worlds are combined in the **pulpit**, the built-in stand-up whirlpool bath hanging out over the bows, whose name derives from the enthusiastic blessings that frequently issue therefrom. Another sacred place is the **lazaret**, a storage tomb between decks into which things (shrouds and such) disappear for days

25. Not to be confused with the land-based structure of the same name, which has no significance to true sailors except for its usefulness in catching exceptionally tall ships attempting to crash harbor parties. (The wobbly thing between the pier and the ship that looks like a movable bridge is a **gangplank**; although one or two people may occasionally fall off it, with careful wobble adjustment the whole gang can be deposited into the water at once.)

◆◆◆

and can only be resurrected by an act of great faith.

Difficulty at sea: some early warning signs.

Great faith is also needed to deal with the problem of alimentation. Food is prepared in the **galley** (short-order kitchen) and served at **mess** (the nautical word for not only "mealtime" but also "what's on the table at meal-time" as well as "what's on the deck a few minutes after mealtime").

On the classiest ships, mess is (wisely) served only a short distance from the **infirmary** ("infirm" being a euphemism for "sick as a dog"; the infirmary was in fact originally called the *sickasadoggery*). Since the nearest hospital may be hundreds of miles away in any one of three hundred and sixty possible directions, anyone with an injury or an illness is invited to wait until the end of his watch and then stagger at his own convenience (with or without the watch) to the infirmary so he can stand in line for three hours in order to have someone half-listen to his symptoms and then sum up his condition with "Ahh, you're not *that* sick," or "Tough it out," or "Ha! Call *that* an injury?"

High above all this is the **crow's-nest**, a place where crows never nest (owing to the fact that it is perpetually full of irritable freezing cold lookouts). The kindest thing that can be said about the crow's-nest is that it commands a fine view of the **poop deck**. (As the name implies, the crows have discovered this, too.)

Where *else* not to go

Since it has recently been established that in certain jurisdictions there *is* peace unto the wicked, at least during the hours of 10 P.M. – 5 A.M., you may find yourself being invited to spend the night in any of a variety of luxurious accommodations: shivering in a berth in a **stateroom**, writhing in a hammock in the **fo'c's'le**, or crouching in the bowels of **steerage**. Which choice is offered to you depends upon how big the ship is, as well as how popular you are with the guys who call themselves your sailing companions.[26]

◆ A *stateroom* is large enough to hold one small bed, one adult, and one toothbrush (if it's not a very big toothbrush). The nearest equivalent on an airplane would be a single-occupancy doggie carrier.

---

26. Truth be told,* a **guy** steadies a spar or sail fore-and-aft and a **companion** is a stairway; the correct term of address for the clowns you spend most of your time with is neither "companions" nor "guys" but "losers," as your other friends will be only too happy to remind you.
* Then again, why start now?

◆ The word *fo'c's'le* can also be spelled *forecastle;* this happens most frequently in the apostrophe-poor countries. The correct pronunciation
   is "folks'll," as in "folks'll laugh at the way you pronounce 'coxswain,' "
   but a good approximation is "foxhole," which is also very apt, since
   it's little more than a hole and it smells suspiciously like a wet
   fox. The nearest equivalent on an airplane would be the forward
   wheel well.

◆ *Steerage* is the traditional class of ticket purchased by Pilgrims, potato
   famine fleers, vast extended families, innocent victims with hearts of gold
   who are sure to drown before the third reel, huddled masses yearning to
   breathe (for a nominal charge, if not actually free), etc. The word "steerage" comes not from the utter inability of the passengers down there to
   steer the ship (in this respect, they are hardly different from the helmsman), but from their tendency to move as a single dense unit and make
   mooing noises.

   The nearest equivalent on an airplane would be to run along behind it.

   An important thing to know about steerage is that there are no locker
   facilities. Passengers are advised to keep their luggage with them at all times.
   In fact, if someone invites you to visit "**Davy Jones's locker**, ha ha," bear in
   mind that this, being a ha ha whimsical term for the ha ha bottom of the
   ocean, is something the careful sailor takes pains never to wind up in. Like

many lockers, it's full of tattered old posters of pinup girls, mildewed gym sneakers, . . . and careless sailors.

How *not* to get there

Giving directions on a boat, if not actually a transcendent experience, is at least a bit like speaking in tongues.

First things first: Resign yourself to the fact that there *is* no place like home.[27] A home has a front and a back, at least a couple of sides, an indoors and an outdoors, maybe an upstairs and a downstairs, possibly some hithers and one or two yons tucked away in a cupboard. Boats have all these things too, but you're not allowed to call them that—that would be too easy. Instead, there is a special set of directional terms reserved for use on boats. Adherence to this word list is an acknowledgment to your listener that you are not at home and helps remind both of you that you are balancing yourselves on a small, cramped, twisting, leaking structure with no fixed position, never more than four miles from the nearest land (although typically it's straight down).

Thus, for instance, although *you* may try to use the word **front** to indicate the pointy end of the boat, *real* sailors only use that word to refer to the bound-

27. And certainly no home like a ship. Even those wacky homes down at the beach—the narrow ones that some tasteless architect has taken great pains to design in the shape of a ship—will never be truly shipshape. The best advice anyone can give those homeowners is "Shape up or ship out."

◆◆◆

ary between two air masses. The "front" of the boat is the **bow** or the **prow** or the **stem**.[28] In the same way, "back" and "behind" are not parts of a boat—they are parts of a sailor. The "back" or "behind" of a boat is the **stern**. If you want to indicate that the garbage cans are behind the front door (which is certainly where we keep them on *my* boat), you may not say that they are "behind the front door." Instead, you must say that they are "abaft the forward hatch."

(On land, of course, **abaft** is something you take in abaftub. At sea there is no concept of personal hygiene, and so the word has become available to mean something entirely different.)

"Abaft" actually comes from the word **aft**, which means "close to or toward the rear of the boat" (assuming you're on the boat to begin with, which, if it's my boat and you don't even know the meaning of *aft*, you aren't). On a possibly interesting side note, if there are two of something on a boat (say, frimlets), and one of them is behind the other, that one is the **after** frimlet. One might think that it is called "after" because it is "more aft" or "closer to aft." However, linguists point out that this theory is not only inexact but also dead wrong. In fact, the frimlet is called "after" because that

◆◆◆

28. No one knows why there are three terms for the same part of the ship (and not a very interesting part, at that). But the terms are not equivalent. *Bow* and *stem* are regular old blue-collar words. *Prow*, on the other hand, is poetic, and in speech is invariably preceded by the word "noble," as in: "the noble prow of the ship." Indeed, "the noble prow of the ship" is such a well-established fixture in nautical literature that laws have been passed governing the use of the phrase. Prows are *always* noble. Why? No one knows. Possibly it is for the same reason that enthusiasm is always unbridled, ringers are always dead, and unction is always extreme.

GLOSSARY

a- *—The all-purpose nautical prefix, meaning variously (depending on context, usage, phase of moon, etc.):*

- *on the*
- *in the*
- *to the*
- *at the*
- *toward the*
- *in a way that kind of reminds some people of a*

- *on*
- *in*
- *to*
- *at*
- *toward*
- *almost—but not exactly— like a*

It thus crams more ambiguity into fewer letters than any other sailing term.

Examples:

- *asleep at the wheel*
- *adrift in the harbor*
- *aground on a sandbar*
- *ashore at some sleazy pub*

is the adjectival construction for "aft," as is well understood by the many thousands of seamen who majored in linguistics.

If another frimlet is brought on board (which is unlikely, frimlets being the rare commodity that they are these days—not like in earlier times) and is placed abaft that after frimlet, this new frimlet is now the **aftmost** frimlet, and not (as might be supposed by ignorant folks who think they aren't) the "aftest" frimlet.

And now that we have all those frimlets on board, if one of those frimlets should happen to fall (**come adrift**) and if it rolls off the boat completely (they usually do) and no one notices (they usually don't), that frimlet will eventually be left **astern** (from

> # GLOSSARY
>
> ## *(a)thwart(ship(s))* —
>
> 1. *From one side of the ship to the other.*
>
> 2. *Inclined to overuse parentheses.*

the root words *as-*, meaning "tail," and *-tern*, meaning "turn"—hence, "to turn tail" [29]). This bodes ill for the ship. Many more ships have sunk due to loose frimlets than for any other reason, with the possible exception of loose lips.

In the other direction, we have **forward** and **ahead**. A common misconception is that these words mean the same thing. This is not the case; *forward* means "toward or closer to the front of the boat"; *ahead* means "in the direction in which the boat (and the screaming passengers) are pointing." The following rule may prove helpful:

◆ A sailor can move *forward,* but a boat never can.

◆ A boat can move *ahead*, but a sailor never can.[30]

The sides of a boat, too, have names, but unlike the sides of a house, which are typically given names like "the side facing mean old Miz Dubil's place" and "the side with the broken window that I just know you're *never* going to get around to fixing," the sides of a boat are given the simple names

---

29. British spelling: *arsetern*.
30. Unless he has relatives in upper management.

port and **starboard**, which equate to "left" and "right." The logic behind calling them something equating to left and right seems to be that if you happen to find yourself facing forward, the side corresponding to left will be on your left and the side corresponding to right will be on your right, which is sensible. The problem, of course, is that you rarely do and they rarely are, so it rarely is.

Difficulty at sea (advanced stages).

As regards indoors and outdoors, note that since the "outdoors" part of a ship is directly over the "indoors" part, the usual way to go outside is to go *up* rather than *out* (plank-walking being the major exception). This is why the traditional words of choice for "indoors" and "outdoors" are not *in* and *out*, but **below** and **above**. (The traditional word of choice for plank-walking is "Aaaaaaaa!")

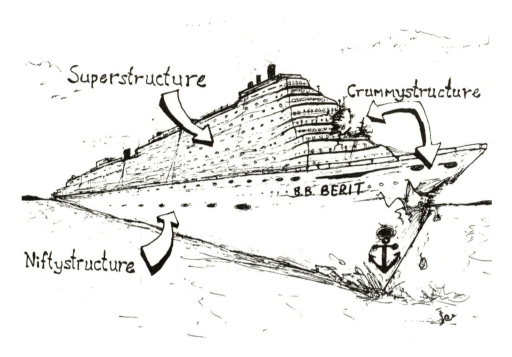

Once you have left the interior of the ship, you are **aboveboard**; that is, out in the open, enjoying the icy salt breeze and the ominous cloud cover and pretending not to hate it all. Its opposite is **belowdecks** (and not *below-board*, as one might expect; in fact, *belowboard* is the opposite of *abovedecks*, in the same way that *gruntled* is the opposite of *underjoyed*).

♦♦♦

With all these confusing extremes, it would appear that the safest place to cower is **amidships**, which is roughly—or precisely, if you insist— halfway between the ends (or the sides) (or the top and bottom) of the ship. *Amidships* is another one of those words that only pretends to be a plural; a common faux pas is for a novice helmsman to respond to the command "Put the helm amidships!" by wrenching off the helm and hurling it squarely amid the nearest group of ships.[31]

♦♦♦

31. But this is as nothing, compared to the embarrassment potential of misinterpreting "Throw me a lifeline, but don't make it fast!" or "I like to cover my privateers with deadeyes, don't you?" or "Blow me down!"

HOW TO TELL
starboard from port
(foolproof method)

An easy way to remember which side of the boat is the starboard side is to perform the following steps (as outlined in the US Navy's indispensable nautical handbook, *The US Navy's Indispensable Nautical Handbook*):

1. Wait for vessel to start moving. (This could take a while.)

2. Face pointy end of same.

3. Pretend to be scanning horizon thoughtfully.

4. Suddenly point into the water (or the sky, or the rigging, or the captain's ear—it doesn't much matter which) and shout hysterically, _____"Limpet mine off the port bow!"

5. Between the moment when vessel jerks sharply to the right (which will, paradoxically, cause it to tilt violently to the left—you will have time later to reflect on this fascinating paradox) and the moment when everyone tumbles into the water, there will be a moment when the boat is practically lying on its side. <u>At that moment,</u> note which side is pointing toward the stars.

6. (Precise timing was important for that previous step.)

7. That side is the starboard side.

Simple.

[Note: Do not attempt this technique if there are no stars.]

[Note: Do not attempt this technique unless you are sure the helmsman already knows what the port bow is, what to do when someone shouts something about a limpet mine off it, etc.]

[Note: Do not attempt this technique too often with the same group of sailing companions.]

USAGE QUIZ #2

1. Which is your favorite nautical term so far—and if not, how frequently? _____
_____

2. Consider this:

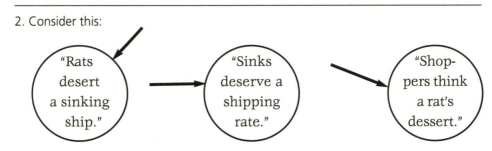

Draw your own conclusions. Now draw someone else's. Color them in.
_____

3. Refer to the following quotation (attributed to Admiral Halsey): "Yer a dog, ye've
   got scurvy, and yer sick as a dog, ye scurvy dog!"
   Discussion points:
   Have you ever owned a scurvy dog?[32] _____
   Do you know anybody who ever owned a scurvy dog?_____
   Given a scurvy dog, what would you consider an appropriate phamacologico-
   veterinary intervention? _____

32. No credit for curvy dogs, scruffy togs, surfer dudes, etc.

◆

4. Remember the *Maine?* Remember the *Pueblo?* What *do* you remember? _____

_____

_____

5. Which of the following is more likely to be found in a car than on a boat?
   - ☐ a. Nagging wife.
   - ☐ b. Whining child.
   - ☐ c. Idiot passenger.
   - ☐ d. Snoozing driver.
   - ☐ e. None of the above.

_____

6. Compose an epic poem in which the majority of the action takes place around:

   ◆   a figurehead _____

       _____

   ◆   a beachhead _____

       _____

   ◆   a masthead _____

       _____

   ◆   a maidenhead _____

       _____

_____

7. If "deck" means "floor" (a place where chairs are traditionally found), then is the
   term "deck chair" ☐ oxymoronic   or ☐ merely redundant?

_____

8. Which of the following body parts is the only one that is not also a nautical term? Be patient.
   ☐ a. throat
   ☐ b. heel
   ☐ c. rib
   ☐ d. uvula

9. Give a precise definition of "a long walk" in relation to the International Yachting and Harbormasters' Association's official definition of "a short pier."_____

10. What combination of the following strikes you as the most poetic?
   ☐ a. bosun on the ocean
   ☐ b. skipper on a clipper
   ☐ c. cox'n with a dachshund
   ☐ d. real big ugly jellyfish with nasty-looking stingers and stuff

11. What does Dr. Spock have to say about the career pressure parents exert on a child when they christen him "Barney Clavell DeSaylor"?

◆◆◆

TANGLY *things*

Oh, what a tangled web we weave,
Recounting where we've been on leave!
—Walt Scott Fitzgerald,
The Old Guy and the Fish

Ever since someone[33] hit upon the idea of tying a few logs together and setting them adrift (with, according to some scholars, his mother-in-law aboard), ropes have been a vital feature of many boats (like baling wire and chewing gum). Knowing The Ropes[34] is as important as Meeting The Quotas, Calling The Shots, and Keeping Up With The Joneses. In fact, there are so many ropes on a ship that until you have learned the function of each and every one of them, you are likely to find yourself serving when you ought to be lashing, paying out when you ought to be making fast, hauling when you ought to be hanging, etc.

The first thing to know is that most ropes are not ropes. What any normal person (and many abnormal people as well) would just call a "rope" is actually a **line**.

◆◆◆

33. Hieronymous Q. Raft, Ph.D.
34. John and Sarah Rope of Teaneck, New Jersey.

◆◆◆

Why? Because.

There is only one rope on a boat whose name actually has the word "rope" in it, rather than the word "line." That rope is the **boltrope**, named in honor of the bolt and the rope, two of the most effective ways of fastening something to something else in an adjustable fashion.[35] To guard against someone's accidentally discovering a use for it, a boltrope is always sewn into the edge of a sail along its entire length, making it virtually impossible to grasp (like so many of these concepts).

Fortunately, other than the boltrope, virtually all of the many lines on a ship bear sensible and predictable names—so much so that upon hearing the name of any line, anyone having the most rudimentary familiarity with the principles of marine construction will instantly be able to describe not only its position but also its function, historical significance, mean time between failures, and/or net depreciated value using the double declining balance method with a mid-quarter convention as appropriate for tangible personal property with a seven-year recovery period. Examples of lines are: **carlines**,MARLINES, *gatlines*, RATLINES, load lines, *COASTLINES*, BUNTLINES, contlines, **streamlines**, CENTER-LINES, *docklines*, **WATERLINES**, ANCHOR LINES, **BUTTOCK LINES**, *heaving lines*, PLIMSOLL LINES, and *hambrolines*. The meanings behind these

◆◆◆

35. It should come as no surprise that the boltrope does not fasten anything to anything else (not even in an adjustable fashion).

names are so obvious that in fact some of them are not lines at all.[36]

Spaces also count (which shows how important it is to read between the lines). For example, a **bowline** is a knot (one word), not a (not one word) **bow line**—although one could, if necessary, tie a bowline on a bow line (or a bowline on a bow tie, or a bow knot on a bowling shoe, or not). It is more usual, however, to tie a bowline on a **bight**. (A *bight,* in other contexts, is either a bay shaped like a bight or a river bend shaped like a bight. In the present context, it is a loop shaped like a bight.)

Thom McAn grew downspout [37]

River bends shaped like bights are not the only kind of bends sailors may encounter. *A* **bend** is also a knot in a line. *The* **bends** is a knot in the tummy.[38] Not every line has a knot in it, but the classiest ones do, and over the last several centuries scores of bends have been invented, all of which can be depended upon to hold securely except when actually desired.

Several flavors of bends belong to the family known as *hitches,* which can

---

36. This carries on the grand tradition of the **chain plank**, which is a metal strap whose utter dissimilarity to both a chain and a plank is nothing short of astonishing.
37. To be sung with an Australian accent.
38. There is also something called a *Benz*, but sailors encounter this only rarely (and sailing instructors, never).

be recognized by their frequent appearance in the best-laid sailing plans. Hitches possess the curious property of being able to hold on for dear life when necessary and yet coming completely apart once the tension is off (exactly like sailing instructors). Examples of hitches are the clove hitch, the half hitch, the taut-line hitch, and the two hitches weekend sailors use most frequently of all: the broken trailer hitch and the -hike hitch.

The formal word meaning "to tie a thing to another thing" is **lash** (not to be confused with the device traditionally used for meting out discipline in the British Navy after rum and sodomy have failed). Given enough rope, virtually anything on a ship can be lashed to anything else. Favorite objects to lash together include:

◆   the tiller to the centerboard;

◆   the life preservers to the beer cooler; and

◆   the captain to the yardarm.

About the only time lashing is to be avoided is when a line is being passed through a hole (or **eye**) in a sail, and then only when the hole has been sewn shut (a "false" eye); technically, even this can be done, but everyone agrees that false-eye lashes are no longer in style.

◆◆◆

How to haul

Rigging is the collective term for all the lines supporting the parts of a boat, or trying to (and as everyone knows, at trying times the lines of support can be crucial). But some lines can be hauled on and some cannot, and it's worthwhile knowing the difference.

All the lines that's fit to haul are called the **running rigging**. (Do not haul on the **running lights**, however, unless you are also intent on **running for your life**). There is an art to safe hauling, and when you are given an order to haul it is not usually sufficient merely to **clap on** (i.e., reach for the nearest convenient part of the nearest convenient line and give it a healthy jerk[39]). The best sailors take the time to determine the answers to Where, How, What, and Which: where to grab the line, how much of a fight it can be expected to put up, what else may come crashing down with it, and which way to run.

Most lines can be thought of as having two sections: the **standing part** and the **fall**. The point of high stress between them (high stress being of course a relative term in this context) is called the **nip**.

> **SURGEON GENERAL'S WARNING:** Prolonged exposure to intricate rigging has been shown to cause annoyance and personal injury in laboratory animals.

---

39. After all, there are always plenty of perfectly healthy jerks on board; who needs another one?

(Naturally, a little nip is recommended whenever stress is high.) The nip is often hard to spot, as it usually hides somewhere in the depths of a **block and tackle**, an arrangement that looks not unlike a hopelessly complicated system of ropes and pulleys and in fact is.[40]

The standing part and the nip are not your concern; the fall is what you will mostly work (and plead) with. But gravity may let you down here,[41] as there is no known logic behind calling the fall the fall. When released (usually inadvertently), the fall does not fall at all but instead promptly shoots up out of reach, wraps itself petulantly around the top of the mast, and like a treed cat or a sulking debutante, refuses to come down for any reason.

A curious result of hauling is that the more you haul, the shorter the standing part will become; at the same time, the fall will get longer. (Note to readers in the Southern Hemisphere: for you the fall will get shorter; this is an indication that winter is on its way.) Do not be alarmed. The total length of the line remains roughly the same.

How *not* to haul

Some of the lines you will encounter—usually in the dark—consist of nothing

---

40. Passengers caught doing The Wave and shouting, "Tackle! Tackle! Block that line!" are missing the point and should be directed toward the shuffleboard courts.
41. As it does everywhere else.

◆◆◆

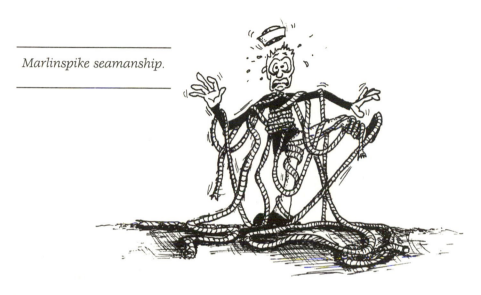

Marlinspike seamanship.

but a standing part. Attempts to haul on these lines are sure to lead to disappointment (disappointment being of course a relative term in this context).

These lines-without-handholds make up the **standing rigging**, which includes such eye-catching (and throat-catching, and back-of-head-catching) features as **stays** and **shrouds**. (The difference between the two is that stays go *this* way, and shrouds go *that* way.) (The expression **in stays** actually means "not moving" and has nothing to do with rigging. Boats are found in stays almost as often as stays are found in boats.)

◆◆◆

For most standing rigging, the material of choice is American standard marine-grade SSCWNSB (Stainless Steel Cable With Nasty Sharp Bits). However, not every steel cable on a ship is part of the standing rigging. **Halyards**, used mostly for dropping sail in a frenetic tizzy at the first whiff of a gust, are often made of SSCWNSB despite (or perhaps on account of) the fact that they are intended to come into contact with human flesh. The pain and suffering thus induced (pain and suffering being of course relative terms in this context) should be welcomed as a character builder.

When it's OK to tie up the line

In a sense, the most important line on a boat is the *bow line,* for this is the boat's leash, and as it goes—when it goes—so goes the rest of the boat. If the goal is to keep the boat from, say, drifting out to sea with no one aboard, then the savvy navvy will take a moment to secure the bow line to something. (The exceptionally savvy navvy will take an additional moment to make sure that the something isn't itself drifting out to sea.)

When throwing a heavy bow line to shore (in the vain hope that some kind passerby will chance upon it, pick it up, and manage to snub it around a piling in time to keep your ship from crunching into someone else's at top speed), bear in mind that eight times out of ten, your throw will fall short and the line will land in the water far from the pier. It is for this reason that the

heaving line was invented: a short, lightweight line attached to the free end of a heavier line. The heaving line, being lighter than the heavier line, can be thrown farther and thus stands a good chance of landing in the water a little closer to the pier.

Small boats have no heaving line but only a short bow line called the **painter**, which is often scarcely long enough to reach the dock (hence the perpetual outcry for longer docks). Additional pitfalls of using short lines to outfit small boats include block tails that come loose and **trucks** (mast caps) that slip down; in fact, all of these are symptoms of the so-called "Tailloose-Lowtruck" (or "short painter") syndrome.

The painter is the true artist of the sea.[42] Sailors occasionally boast about how wonderful sails are and how well they can draw, but basically, they are just windbags. And the only thing the rest of the boat can draw is water, which is determined by whether it's sticking down below the surface a little

42. For no known reason, painters have long been a favorite nautical theme. The lyrics of the Top-40 chantey "Sloop John B." describe how

> Poor Kupka, he caught the Fitz*
> And threw away all the Magrittes

and, after the first mate got drunk and began looting a trunk full of Impressionist masterpieces:

> Constable had de Kooning take a Manet.

*Evidently a reference to a ship immobilized in another classic sea ballad, "The Wreck of the *Ella Fitzgerald*."

bit or a lot. The more the boat draws, the deeper it tends to immerse itself in its medium—like a slightly fanatical, slightly unstable art student.

On the other hand, a *small* increase in the underwater percentage of the boat often improves its stability—specifically its **ultimate stability**, or tendency to stay right-side up. Ultimate stability can also be achieved by other means, such as running aground or never putting the boat in the water in the first place. In fact, for *ultimate* ultimate stability, a wise skipper simply **scuttles** his boat (i.e., sinks it and then scuttles away across the floor of the silent sea). Sinking the boat guards against capsizing in the same way heavy drinking guards against injury: to wit, You Can't Fall Off The Floor.

Keeping LINES *in line*

The commotion attending a line gone astray has led to the invention of lines whose only function is to keep other lines from escaping. Collaborators of this sort (reviled by their fellow lines) are called **jackstays** or **tiedowns**.[43]

But beyond that, there aren't many things that can be done with lines, apart from tugging, flinging, fastening, and stringing (e.g., ~ up Billy Budd). And yet, because of their vital importance to the functioning of a ship (and to

43. As of this writing, a consortium of really industrious shipbuilders is developing new lines whose function will be to keep jackstays and tiedowns from escaping. These will probably be called either *jackstaystays* or *tiedown tiedowns*.

the bottom lines of the annual financial statements of marine cordage manufacturers), and also because it's well known that every sailor needs an outlet
for his maternal instinct, lines are among the best cared-for parts of any ship.
They even have their own covers, which are tied onto them via the three-step
process of **worming**, **parceling**, and **serving**. This procedure has been
developed for foul-weather protection[44] and should not be confused with the
three-step process of decontaminating, packaging, and feeding dog meat to
the crew (at what has come to be known as "Chow time").

GLOSSARY

she—
1. *Your boat.*
2. *Your wife.*

She—My *wife.*

---

44. Now standard police procedure, as indicated by the police motto: "to protect and to serve."

EQUAL OPPORTUNITY *for the* UNFIT

Befuddled by all these new unfamiliar meanings for old familiar words? Beginning to suspect that virtually any word in English, no matter how irrelevant, can be (and has been) wrestled into employment in the nautical jargon? Annoyed when people leave words off the start of a question?

Then you are a person of rare perception.[45]

---

45. You can be certain this is being said in earnest; there's no need to butter you up falsely at this point, as you've already bought the book.

In fact, independent laboratory research has confirmed that the only words in the language that have *not* been appropriated for use at sea are:

Those *with*

EXCEPTIONALLY

STRAIGHTFORWARD,

simple,

unambiguous

MEANINGS.

This is a good rule of thumb (something that ought to go directly from the tip of your tongue into everyone's ear).

WRINKLY *things*

Aboard! Aboard! For shame!
The wind sits in the shoulder of your sail
And you are stayed for.
—Polonius in *Hamlet* (too busy mangling the nautical
   anatomy to notice that he has ended three out of four
   sentences with a preposition)

To sail—an extraordinary occurrence named after the miraculous object that makes it possible—can be defined as "not to go nowhere in a sailboat." When all is going well (to speak hypothetically for a moment), the sails will be up, taut, filled, and in general no great embarrassment. How to get them that way is a matter of the utmost importance. However, as the process of rigging a sailboat is essentially akin to making a four-dimensional bed in the shower using only your elbows, it cannot possibly be elucidated in such a short book. We will therefore dispense with the instructions and assume that someone else has put up the sails for you.[46]

---

46. If you yourself are in fact the sad individual to whose lot it has fallen to put up the sails, you'll need additional resources beyond this one book. Why not buy a second copy? It's just possible that you'll learn twice as much.

◆◆◆

Now that the blithe assumptions have been made and the sails are up, and while the boat is still safely (though menacingly) riding at anchor, let's take a brief tour of the sails and assess the damage.

One curious point is that the word "sail" is very rarely heard in its entirety, despite its brevity and the pivotal role the sails play in sailing (as compared with the **rudder**, which plays the pivotal role in pivoting). Diligent philological analysis of speech samples taken from everyday shipboard conversations (the printable excerpts) has revealed that the word "sail" is in fact constantly present (and bandied about in the badinage with almost bantering abandon), but that it is not being given its full complement of vowels, especially when it has another word stuck to its forehead. Thus, the *mainsail* is not voiced as the "maaain saaail"—it is simply (and brusquely) the "mains'l." Similarly, a *foresail* is a "fores'l" (not "fooore saaail," a drawling mispronunciation which invariably elicits the question, "How much are you aaaaasking?"), the *topsail* is the "tops'l," and the *headsail* is the "heads'l."[47] Unless you learn to swallow your vowels (approx. cal.: 60), you won't be the only one who has no idea what you're talking about.

As a matter of fact, you can use the fact that sails have first names to your advantage. When someone asks you to point out "the topsail," you know that it has something to do with "top," which tells you that you will find it by looking up (or by looking it up). When he mentions "the mainsail," you know you

◆◆◆

47. Pronunciation guide: "heads'l" rhymes with "Edsel" (and is only slightly less obsolete).

will find it by looking on the mainmast. When he mentions "the foresail," you know you will find it by first locating a forestay or a foremast; the foresail is then usually close by, half of it draped across the deck and the other half trailing in the water.

On the other hand, there are not many clues in the word **jib** to help you find the jib, which turns out to be a forward sail. And when asked to locate something as exotic as the **genoa jib**, many novices reveal their noviceness by looking in the general direction of Genoa.

Any shape you want . . . as long as it's a ☐

In earlier times, all sails were square, and most ships needed at least three of them for day sailing (the so-called "three squares a day"). At some point, the world's shipyards switched tacks and began producing triangular sails. What caused this change to come about? Fashion designers, runs one conjecture; but this does not jibe with the theory that by slicing each square into two tri-angles, the sailmakers may simply have been trying to double production. (It was well known that the Germans had been working on a way to convert one square sail into two: one made from the front side, the other from the back. They later abandoned this effort, having reached the conclusion that a ship rigged with one-sided sails could only go one way.)

The sudden move to triangular sails meant that customers who had prepaid for four corners would now receive only three. Riots broke out in the southwestern United States[48] when consumers angrily began demanding that fourth corner anyway. Only when the manufacturers agreed to start warehousing their leftover corners and making them available for discount purchase was peace restored.[49] The entire recreational boating after-market began to shift toward surplus sail parts, particularly edges and corners. Eventually, the market shifted away from the edge and rallied exclusively around the corner, creating a new prosperity (since, after all, that's just where prosperity has always been).

One advantage of using three-edged sails is that there is one less word for neophyte sailors to have to learn. (This is in fact the sole advantage of using three-edged sails.)[50] The words that remain are predictably inaccurate. The **leech**, for example, is the free edge of the sail: no one can deny the unmistakable parasitic charm of the word, and yet unlike its bloodsucking relative (easily confused with a brother-in-law—brother-in-law being a relative term in this context), the leech is the one thing *not* attached to anything. In this same vermin vein, **roaches** might be expected to look like leeches on legs but are actually curves on leeches. (Curves on legs are something else again.)

A sail's effectiveness has something to do with its shape and size. Govern-

48. Near Four Corners, as a matter of fact.
49. This was the first known instance of marketing the corner.
50. To date, the movement to adopt the *two*-edged sail has posted rather disappointing results.

ment-funded research has shown conclusively that a love triangle feels more
crowded than Times Square on New Year's Eve. This implies that a triangle
is more crowded than a square, from which it can be extrapolated that all
triangular sails are smaller than all square sails. Sailmakers struggling

to keep the math simple have therefore developed the geometrical concept of the **aspect ratio**, which is the quotient of proportionality yielded when one divides the perpendicular extent of a triangular sail by what the width would have been if it were to have equaled the arithmetic mean of the extremes of its dispersion. Apart from filling space in sailing guides and research grant proposals, this is of no practical value whatsoever—but it does make a great conversation stopper.

Everybody's *watching*

Sails are visible from rather a long way away, and this feature makes them quite useful as a method of telegraphing to the rest of the world the complete lack of nautical expertise aboard. The most common signal that no one in the crew knows what he's doing is **luffing** (or crying). The **luff** of a triangular sail is the forward edge (unless you've done it wrong); when it flaps idly in the breeze, this is an unmistakable indication that *somebody* hasn't been paying att*entionnnn*. . . . However, flapping idly in the breeze is universally recognized as the prerogative of sails, so there is no need for apology.[51]

Another common activity of sails is the maneuver known as **jibing**, during which every sail on the boat shifts suddenly and violently to the opposite

---

51. Which is why luff means neffer haffing to say you're sorry.

side of the boat. (Some boats have a **jibing centerboard**, which of course has nothing to do with jibing.) This abrupt flip-flap-flop of the sails is difficult to hide from the view of onlookers, as is the concomitant loss of life.

There is also the risk of an unintentional **goosewing**, in which a boom catches in a backstay or a sail gets completely fouled up in a spreader.[52] (The unrelated term **goosewinged** is an allegedly intentional maneuver per-formed when the wind is due aft; it begins with the mainsail on one side of the boat and the foresail on the other and ends with a boom caught in a back-stay or a sail completely fouled up in a spreader. Do not confuse this with the **gooseneck**, which is the joint holding the boom to the mast and which resembles nothing so remotely as it does a gooseneck lamp or a goose's neck. Whoever named *goosewing, goosewinged,* and *gooseneck* must have failed Goose Anatomy 101. The reason we are grousing is that this turkey obviously ducked his responsibility. Perhaps he was chicken and quailed at unpheasant thoughts.)[53]

The more violent aspects of sailing can be abated somewhat by **reefing**, or reducing the amount of sail exposed to the wind. There are several tech-niques for accomplishing this; one of the less destructive choices is **roller reefing** (rolling up the sail partway on the boom). Without actually contribut-ing anything to blunt the impact of the boom against the cranium, roller reef-

52. Top marks for artistic expression, but zero for technical merit.
53. Feel free to cry fowl.

ing does aid in keeping the boat downside-down. (Reefer rolling has the opposite effect.) The downside is that careless reefing may result in a sail that is sheeted in too tight, causing it to **stall**. This phenomenon became the subject of several documentary shorts in the 1930's by film pioneer Leni Reef'n'stall.

When all else fails, you can **douse** the sail, which means to take it down suddenly, whether or not it's on fire.[54]

Three sheets, no wind

For all it owes to aeronautical engineering and fluidics, sailing is still the art of catching air in a bag.[55] To pay homage to these roots, ships still carry sails reminiscent of big pillowcases, which can be used to catch just a little more breeze (or a few more Z's). The **spinnaker** is the best-known example of such a sail, although a more generic term is **ballooner**, which is also a term for a person traveling in a hot-air balloon (and laughing at sailors because *they* are at the mercy of wind, weather, and waves, while *he* is only at the mercy of wind and weather).

A particular type of ballooner is the **gollywobbler**; it was formerly called the **main-topmast balloon staysail** until someone pointed out how silly that sounded.

54. It usually is.
55. Like vacuuming, from which it is distinguished mostly by the scarcity of dust bunnies.

◆◆◆

Unlike most other sails, the spinnaker is attached to a spar from which it must be periodically disconnected. This allows the crew to jibe the spinnaker in either of two ways: the **end-for-end jibe**, which is suitable for a person sure-footed enough to hold a pole in one hand without beaning himself, or the **dip-pole jibe**, which is suitable for the rest of us.

Oversized spinnakers are generically called **parachutes**, which is what a hot-air balloon with a deep gash turns out to be a poor substitute for (and that's when the sailors get their revenge).

Non-sails

Some of the things that flap in the wind aren't sails at all. Sometimes they are jaws, but usually they are **flags** and **pennants**, which can be distinguished from sails by the absence of sailors cursing at them.

Dipping an ensign is a form of salute (when it means lowering a flag of nationality) or a form of amusement (when it means submerging a junior officer). Submerging a junior officer is frowned upon as a juvenile and petty prank chiefly engaged in by officers who are themselves petty.

Pride in yacht-club membership (and proof of the payment of exorbitant membership fees) is displayed by flying a **burgee**, which is a yacht-club pennant (or any similar object likewise designed to be burged by a burger).

ICKY *things*

Break, break, break,
On thy cold gray stones, O Sea!
And I would that my willpower could hold back
The meal that arises in me.
—Andrew Lloyd Tennyson,
Break, Break, Break, . . . Breakfast!

Icky things on a boat can be divided (when it is absolutely impossible to avoid thinking about them any longer) into two classes: those that can be avoided, and those that cannot.

Eeeeeuuuuwwww . . .

Icky things that *can* be avoided include:

◆   anything having to do with fish; and

◆   anything having to do with food.

Avoiding fish is a fairly simple two-step process:

1. Stay off fishing boats.

2. Don't fall into the water.

Avoiding food is more counterintuitive, until you've had your first meal or tried to use the head during particularly violent weather.

Icky things that *cannot* be avoided can all be blamed on Sir Isaac Newton. Gravity operates at sea in approximately the same direction as it does on land, and icky things, tending to be denser and slipperier than non-icky things, invariably gravitate toward the lowest points in the ship. For this reason, it is important to avoid the low points during your trip (low points being of course a relative term in this context).

> ## GLOSSARY
>
> **seasick**—*Early indication that it's time to stop all this nonsense and get back on dry land.*
>
> **seizure**—*Late indication that it's time to stop all this nonsense and get back on dry land.*

DOUBLE E*eeeeuuuu*WWWW . . .

Two low points especially to avoid are the hold and the bilge. As the main storage area for cargo, the **hold** is more or less the *raison d'être* (or "raisin-to-be"; i.e., grape) of the ship. By analogy with Hell (from which the word *hold* is undoubtedly derived), a hold should be a clean, well-lighted place, but it is not. This is partly due to the presence of icky things placed in it recently (green bananas, slabs of whale blubber, 55-gallon drums of untreated fertilizer, etc.), and partly because of the presence of icky things placed in it a long time ago (colonies of rats, rotten bananas, leftover whale-blubber sandwiches, etc.). The icky things in the hold are kept from sticking together by **dunnage**, which is a catch-all term for "cargo packing material" (usually consist-

> ## GLOSSARY
>
> **hold**—*An empty space in the hull; the larger the better.*
>
> **hole**—*An empty space in the hull; the smaller the better.*
>
> **hull**—*The collection of nautical material surrounding a variety of empty spaces.*

ing of straw, plastic foam peanuts, and third-class passengers).

The **bilge** claims the distinction of being the without-question hands-down yuckiest part of the boat, bar none.[56] All the dirty, slimy, smelly, foul, putrid, fetid seawater (not to mention the seawater that isn't so nice) that has been sloshing around in the boat since time immemorial eventually trickles its way down through the ship's nooks and crannies and into the bilge. It trickles its way back out via the **bilge pump**, but bilge pumps tend to jam. Along came the bilge-pump strainer, whose inventor struck a chord with the public

56. As voted by an overwhelming majority of the ballots cast in the 1958 Yucky Boat Part Elections.

◆◆◆

by nicknaming it the **strum box**, perhaps in an attempt to distract attention from the fact that putting a strainer on a bilge pump is a sure-fire way to get all the nice clean water out of the bilge while keeping only the most revolting chunks of stuff in.

Bilge has a double meaning; it is also the term for the contents *of* the bilge. Here we have an excellent example of a grammatical *metonymy*, one which might cause some amount of confusion, but frankly, if the conversation stalls over the meaning of *bilge,* maybe it's time to find a new topic—or a new group of friends.

USAGE QUIZ #3

1. Which of the following belongs with the others?
    - ☐ a. tops'l
    - ☐ b. mains'l
    - ☐ c. sprits'l
    - ☐ d. guided mis'l
    - ☐ e. Hans'l und Gret'l

___

2. Develop a fully satisfactory method of inventory-based accounting which would be applicable to the cargo packing material used in a ship carrying a cargo of . . . cargo packing material. Defend it in Tax Court._____

___

3. How much would you pay for an autographed picture of:
    - a. Hal Yard? $ _____
    - b. Stan Chen? $ _____
    - c. Jack Stay? $ _____
    - d. Otto Pilate? $ _____
    - e. Sue Na'ami? $ _____
    - f. Bill O'Leighden? $ _____

___

4. If the fullness of a sail is called "draft," and the fullness of a sail is also called "belly," then what is the precise etymological relationship between "draft" and "belly"? Points will be deducted for failing to notice the relationship between "draft beer" and "beer belly." _____

5. In a darkish dankish swankish Turkish nightclub, have you ever found yourself dancing (in rapid succession):
   ☐   1) the Close Reach?
   ☐   2) the Senhouse Slip?
   ☐   3) the Turnbuckle?
   ☐   4) the Touch and Go?
   ☐   5) the Tumblehome?

6. What's that thing bobbing in the ocean . . . ahead?_____

7. Rewrite the following, ten times fast (with gusto):
   Suzanne can run out and haul on an outhaul; board and rig out an outrigger; haul out, rig, and run an outboard; and holler, "Runner boarding!", hauling running rigging; but her border collie, Holly, can outrun her, out-board her, out-haul her, out-holler her, and out-rig her. _____
   _____
   _____

8. Which of the following reminds you of the others, and who?
   - ☐ a. Man overboard.
   - ☐ b. Mind over matter.
   - ☐ c. π over 2.
   - ☐ d. Pittsburgh over St. Louis.

9. If you could drive just one of the boats James Bond gets to drive . . . how cool would *that* be?_____

   _____

10. Any time you find yourself sailing briskly along on a sparkling sea with the sun bright, the breeze fresh, and the helm responding to the gentlest of touches, you should:
    - ☐ a. Keep 'er steady as she goes.
    - ☐ b. Fall off to a beam reach and plot a course for the nearest beacon.
    - ☐ c. Hoist the spinnaker, ease the main, and hike out on the windward gunwale.
    - ☐ d. Pinch yourself and wake up.

11. Does *your* love have any use for a boxing glove ten thousand miles away? Don't catch that morning train unless you're sure.

    _____

    _____

◆◆◆

INVISIBLE *things*

A wet sheet and a flowing sea,
A wind that follows fast:
Our first motel at Waikiki
Will also be our last.
—Allan Come-again,
The Soggy Scotsman

In sailing, as in most of the rest of this wretched existence, what you see is what you get. There are only two exceptions to this rule—two things that you get although you *can't* see them. These are: aggravation and wind.

Nothing can be done about either one.

However, as the entire rest of this book has been devoted to discussing aggravation, let's now take a moment to turn our attention to the wind.

Everyone's nose is windy

Although man has been harnessing the power of the wind for millennia (and dogs have been hanging their heads out car windows for slightly longer than that), it is only recently that anyone has taken the time to

GLOSSARY

apparent wind—
True wind plus the vector which is antiparallel to (but of the same magnitude as) the vector describing the boat's motion. Can be calculated with complete accuracy by simple application of the Theory of Relativity.

develop a vocabulary of the wind. Where once sailors used phrases like, "The wind's veering to the right," and "The wind's veering to the left," and "Stand downwind, will ya, fellah?", it is now more common to hear them say breezy things like, "Wind's **veering**," and "Wind's **backing**," and "Not *up*wind—*down*wind!", and it is only after puzzled looks have been exchanged all around that they will revert in exasperation to: "*Veering* means veering to the right," and "*Backing* means veering to the left," and "What, do you need help spelling *P.U.?*"

Unfortunately, being able to discuss what the wind is doing is not the same as being able to make use of that information. Getting a sailboat to accelerate requires some amount of knowledge encompassing more than just where the wind is, where the boat is, and why never the twain shall meet.[57] In any case, the **accelerator** is not a pedal but a chemical used to make fiberglass, and accelerating is accomplished not by "stepping on the gas" (which will only result in highly volatile footwear) but by combining the Three Principal Elements of legend:

57. Answer: Because it was wate weaving the station.

1. Wind.

2. Intelligence.

3. A dearth of large rocks directly in front of the boat.

Modern sailors are finally starting to get a handle on the wind. The issues of intelligence and large rocks have been left to future millennia.

And they *call the wind* Marina

The Twentieth Century,[†] epoch of technological wonders that it turned out to be,[58] has produced two miracles unmatched in human history:

1. an explanation of how a boat can sail into the wind (something about parallelograms and Bernoulli); and

2. a device for making wind visible.

A full discussion of the physics of sailing into the wind is beyond the scope of this book,[59] but the device for making wind visible is the well-known **telltale**. The exact principles by which it works are protected by patents, but put sim-

---

† R.I.P.
58. Super Nintendo, morning drive-time radio, Fascism, etc.
59. Because it is beyond the scope of this author.

ply, it is an apparatus constructed from a quantity of fibrous ovine excrescent material in coaxial helical arrangement, one terminus of which is affixed apposite to a stay, the other of which is subject to a plurality of degrees of positional and rotational freedom. The system constantly seeks to minimize its own potential with respect to the surrounding atmospheric pressure differential, and the helmsman's precise observations of the resulting transitions between local equilibria are vulgarly known as "seein' where th' scrap o' yarn's pointin'."

But fear not, O conservative stalwarts: Every piece of technology has its antidote, and the telltale is no exception. Two forces can conspire to render the telltale useless:

1. Sunset (happens approximately once per day).

2. Dead calm (happens all the bloody time).

Sunset (also known as "red sky at night") is the sailor's name for the traditional ceremony marking the start of several hours of completely random wandering in the dark (also known as "sailor's delight"). Fortunately, every sunset is followed (eventually) by a **sunrise**. This is the sailor's name for the traditional ceremony marking the start of several hours of completely random wandering in the light.

Dead calm is characterized by a complete lack of wind. Sailors being the nervous sorts they are, their calmness will typically vary in inverse proportion to the wind's.

◆◆◆

Do not mistake a lack of **apparent wind** for dead calm. Apparent wind (closely related to wind-chill factor) approaches zero as the **boat** falls off (i.e., turns farther away from the direction from which the wind is blowing). Incidentally, *falling off* is the only maneuver that both precedes and follows a jibe. First the boat does it . . . then the crew does it.

But *the wind cries* Marty

All boats have two **rails** (one on each side), and at any given moment the wind (if there is any) will be making its entrance over one (the **windward rail**) and exiting over the other (the **lee rail**). It is important to discern which is which, as the windward rail possesses the unique property that anything put on or over it (e.g., garbage,

Force	Clew	Description	Advice for sailors
THE BUFORD SCALE OF WIND VELOCITY			
0		Not enuf wind	Not worth the effort—stay home
1	,,	,,	,,
2	,,	,,	,,
3	,,	,,	,,
4	,,	,,	,,
5		2 much wind	Not worth the risk — stay home
6	,,	,,	,,
7	,,	,,	,,
8	,,	,,	,,
9	,,	,,	,,
10	,,	,,	,,
11		homes flattened	No HOME—might as well go sailing

◆◆◆

cigarette butts, the captain) always comes back on board immediately. The lee rail works in the exact opposite way: anything put there instantly makes a beeline for Portugal.

FDA NOTICE

The lee rail is the only rail approved for use by patients desiring to communicate with Ralph, the patron saint of Dramamine withdrawal.

Normally, the mainsail will be found flapping annoyingly somewhere near the lee rail. However, in defiance of Newton's laws, defiant sailors (and Newton's lawyers) have occasionally been able to get it to flap annoyingly somewhere near the *windward* rail; this is called **sailing by the lee** (or, alternatively, **sailing like a damn fool**) and is just about guaranteed to lead to a **flying jibe** (which is the sailor's euphemism for a jibe that no one—not even Newton—was expecting).

Example:

"Holy *cow,* skipper! Did you just jibe accidentally?"

"Er . . . no . . . er, that was intentional. It's, ah, what we call a 'flying jibe.' "

"Oh. . . . Well. So why don't you climb back on board and let's get going?"

❖❖❖

MAGICAL *things*

Columbus sailed the ocean, blue,
In fourteen hundred ninety-two.
For many weeks he was at sea
Complaining, "Where the heck *are we?"*
—Anne Aughn, M.S.,
Good Boy, Columbus

Granted, there have been scattered unsubstantiated rumors of boats that reach their final destinations without major mishap, but contrary to the way it may appear, this is rarely due to luck, fate, faith in the Almighty, or sheer blessed ignorance. Nor can time, tide, physics, or the laws of wind and wave be blamed. No, the truth is that boats are operated, purely and simply, by: black magic.

Black magic is what makes a boat end up not far from where you actually thought it was going to go; black magic is what keeps it from foundering on a daily basis; and black magic is what made you go aboard *this* time because you forgot all about what it was like to be aboard *last* time.

Most of this black magic takes place in the chart room, where the cabalist's tools and instruments can be safely hidden away from the prying eyes of mere mortals. It is to this sacrosanct sanctum sanctorum that the practitioner of the ancient arts retires when he senses that the time is nigh to call forth the spirits of the vasty deep and ask for their assistance (or, more frequently, bribe them with the promise of sacrificial human reflux).[60]

Double, double *toilet* trouble

The primary tool of the nautical necromancer's craft is the **chart**. Charts, which look astonishingly like what sensible people have always been content to call *maps,* are usually sold in large collections bound into thick books. A complete set of charts can cover enormous expanses of the globe—everywhere, in fact, except where you are at the moment.

Nautical charts are printed with colored inks whose variegated hues are rivaled only by those of rainbows, stamps, and subway graffiti. The standard colors were chosen for their ability to resist fading and defy common sense. For instance, the color white is used to represent the open ocean (which is blue in real life—at least, in fourteen hundred ninety-two it was, according to one reliable historical resource). By the same logic, blue ink means something green (shallow water), green means yellow (beaches), and yellow means gray (concrete).

60. In extreme cases when it was necessary to appease the spirits of navigation to avoid wrecking, actual humans have been sacrificed (preferably those whom nobody likes very much, e.g., the navigator). This is the origin of **dead reckoning**.

In this spirit of color-blindness, it is considered perfectly acceptable to purchase charts by offering Monopoly money.

When traveling from point A to point B, bear in mind that the main difference between a chart and a map is that the map will give many useless details, such as the population of point A and the elevation above sea level of the steps of City Hall in point B. In contrast, the chart will say nothing at all about points A and B but will instead display an almost fanatical obsession with points C, D, E, F, G, H, and any other points in between. This reflects the sailor's belief (not shared by Columbus) that the trip is more important than the destination.

Typical navigation scenario.

The most important fact communicated by charts is exactly how deep the water is (what might be called *elevation below sea level*). Water depth is important to sailors not because they plan to go diving, but so that in case they aren't given a say in the matter, they will know how long it will take them to reach bottom. Depth is measured in **fathoms** rather than in feet or meters. One fathom (six feet) was chosen as the standard unit possibly because, being one armspan, it is easy to measure along a rope—or possibly because, being the average height of a man, it represents the minimum depth required to keep the wiseguy's head from bobbing back to the surface of the East River.

Of course, the depth of the ocean is changing all the time, mostly due to the effects of tide, evaporation, global warming, people leaving the water running while they brush their teeth, etc., so the numbers on charts are averages and should only be used for comparison. Your fathomage may vary.

Faster than a *breeding* pullet

Black magic is required not only to figure out where to go but also how long it will take to get there. Ships being the slightly-less-than-instantaneous modes of transport that they are, it can sometimes take an appreciable (or disparage-able) number of seconds to travel from point A to point B.

Travel time is inversely proportional to the speed of the boat. (Compare this with a car, where travel time is proportional to the quantity of Pepsi the

◆◆◆

kids have consumed.) The speed of a boat, like the condition of its passengers' stomachs, is measured in **knots**. A knot is one **nautical mile** per hour, and a nautical mile is a distance equaling 6,076 feet (one mile plus tax and tip). The reason a nautical mile is bigger than a not-nautical (or *statuesque*) mile (and this is true everywhere on the earth, not just in Texas) is that a nautical mile equals one minute of arc, and a minute of arc is easy to measure on the ocean: you simply observe (if possible) the stars (if possible) at night (if possible).[61]

To keep the trip from being over too soon, Nature in her indefinite wisdom has provided a built-in speed regulator: the **hull speed**, the theoretical maximum waterspeed of the boat's hull (and, if all goes well, of the rest of the boat, too). Hull speed depends on the LWL (or **load waterline length**), the length of the loaded boat where it intersects the water (or vice versa), so a longer boat tends to have a higher hull speed.[62] Still, it is not automatically true that the longer the hull, the less time the trip will take,[63] although it *is*

61. Don't worry too much about distances. A **long ton** really isn't much longer than a regular ton, and nothing on a **12-meter boat** measures 12 meters.
62. The boat itself may of course be much longer than the LWL; the LOA (or **length overall**) is the length of the entire boat and everyone and everything on it—including their overalls— except not quite: it does not necessarily include the pointy bits sticking off both ends. Ripped raft gift wrap at tip-top ship shops and specious steerage storage space specs bear witness to this truth, as many tears have been shed (and sheds have been torn) as a result of failing to take the pointy bits into account.
63. As will be tested late next year in the eagerly awaited *QEII*-vs.-Boogie-Board Transatlantic Regatta.

always true that no matter how much speed you pour on, the folks up front will still manage to get there first (except in the case of backwatering, also known as "traveling **sternforemost**," which is a translation of the Danish *båsse-øckveoords*).

The hull speed is (naturally) equal to:

$$k \times \sqrt{\text{LWL}} \mid 1.2 \text{ arc-min./hr.-ft.}^{\frac{1}{2}} \lesssim k \lesssim 1.7$$

$$k_{\text{disp.}} = 1.34 \text{ (of course).}[64]$$

(The hull speed formula is exceeded in complexity only by the Thames Measurement formula:

$$(L - B) \times \tfrac{1}{2} B^2 / 94$$

which is useful mainly for measuring the Thames.)

The use of the familiar letter k here instead of some other, scarier letter (like x, or ¢, or ®) is purely arbitrary and should in no way be viewed as any sort of concession to those of us who don't speak calculus. Particularly since the k stands for "konstant." Mathematicians are like that.

A **planing boat** (but not a **displacement boat**), can go faster than its hull speed (known as **surfing**, or **driving like a lunatic**), but it will konstantly

---

64. This from the same people who decreed that there are only *two* quarters in a ship. Those of you who were led to believe that there would be no math in this class may claim your refunds at the door.

find itself climbing up the back side of the wave created by its own prow, which is a bit like driving your car up a tree from the back seat. For some mysterious reason, though the boat climbs and climbs, it never rises above the surface of the ocean. In fact, the moment it slows down, the prow wave will overtake it from behind, leaving the frustrated (and damp) skipper to curse his prow (or, for female skippers, prowess).

It wasn't long before someone (possibly the legendary harbor pilot Billy Bob Einstein) actually worked his way through all of that math and realized that the maximum speed of the boat does depend on the length after all (though not overall), which is why the boogie board in next year's regatta is being designed to be thirty-seven miles long.

I CAN TELL YOU *where* TO GO, BUT I CAN'T TELL YOU *how* TO GET THERE

Long ago charts were indispensable, but these days most of the real navigating is done by impersonal electronic gadgets (autopilots, GPS, radar, VHF, Mission Control, etc.). Still, a wise navigator should be proficient in the use of the time-honored charting tools so that he can, in time of crisis, make himself appear terribly busy. The most important tools are **dividers** (which do not divide anything and which cannot be separated: one divider is about as useful as one scissor), **parallel rules** (a precision instrument which makes it possible to plot a course that is wrong by *exactly* 180 degrees), and **matches** (for

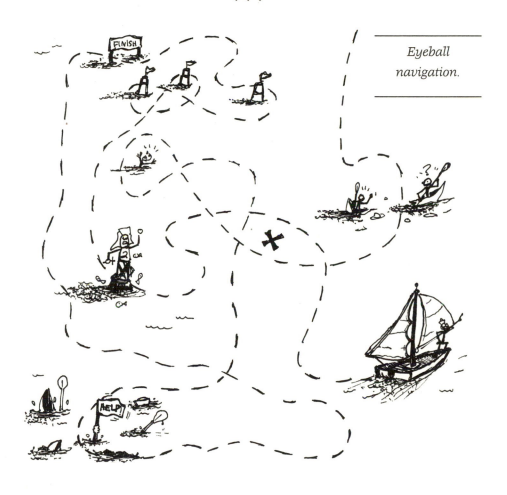

Eyeball navigation.

◆◆◆

those cold winter nights when charts are the only thing left to burn).

Results of the navigator's black magic computations are communicated to the helm (or to the people on it, if any and if conscious), and the course is adjusted accordingly (if deemed worth it). The results of these course adjustments are later recorded in the **log**, the official book in which all the most embarrassing moments of each cruise are memorialized for the mockery of future generations.

Most log entries conclude with the navigator's standard notation *Limited Observations, Still Tabulating*—or its abbreviation.

No matter where you go, . . .

All of this black magic, of course, is only necessary because navigation is traditionally the province of men.

If a woman were in charge, she would simply pull over and ask for directions.

UNEQUIVOCALLY *ambiguous* TERMINOLOGY

There is no Frigate like a Book
To take us Lands away —
With Luggage too, though, I'da took
The Frigate — any Day —
—Emptily Dickensian,
Boats Is Better 'cause Books Gets Wetter

There are four nautical terms that, for no very good reason and without any apology, have been appropriated to mean so many different things that they are now almost meaningless. These four are **trim**, **board**, **tack**, and **port**, and despite their now almost meaninglessness, you are now going to learn them.

GLOSSARY

board—*Get onto a boat, against one's better judgment.*
-board—*All-purpose term meaning "having anything to do with boats."*
bored—*All-purpose term meaning "having anything to do with boats."*

Trim

This bit of triminology, meaning "adjust" or "adjustment," has now found its way into the following common expressions:

trim a sail—Adjust a sail, positioning it to catch all the wind there isn't.

trim of a sail—Angle between a sail and the place the wind isn't coming from.

trim of the boat—Angle of the boat to the water (easily measured by checking sneaker dampness).

trim the boat—"Move your butt before we capsize, you moron—can't you see how wet my sneakers are getting?!"

Board

Board (as in **on board**, meaning "on or onto a ship"[65]) is an especially insidious word (although it can be found outsidious on nice days) because it appears not only on its own but also hanging around the ends of other words. In fact, although great handfuls of terms contain the suffix *-board,* only a few of them have anything to do with any particular board, or with multiple boards, or indeed with wood in general. Most of them have to do with location relative to the boat. Naturally.

65. I.e., miserable.

This absurd substitution of one common word for a more precise word (a time-honored tradition in English, as evidenced by the whatchamacallits and thingummies of various so-and-so's) can be traced back to the days when boats were little more than collections of boards—and, given the state of navigation at the time, were constantly being reduced to their constituent boards again. The word *boat* itself may come from the word *board,* altered through the action of a now archaic verb-modal substantive functional shift; an approximate rendering in modern English might be "the once and future board."

As an example of the widespread appearance of the suffix *-board,* consider the following terms:

◆ **INBOARD** ◆ onboard ◆ *outboard* ◆ **overboard** ◆

◆ ABOVEBOARD ◆ *CENTERBOARD* ◆ DAGGERBOARD ◆ ***aboard*** ◆

◆ SHIPBOARD ◆ **duckboard** ◆ SEABOARD ◆ LEEBOARD ◆

◆ FREEBOARD ◆ *starboard* ◆ LARBOARD ◆ *garboard* ◆

To save time and brain space (two highly precious commodities, even for sailors), the novice seaman would do well not to clutter his mind with the *-board* part at all, but simply to memorize the meanings of **in**, **on**, **out**, **over**, **above**, **center**, **dagger**, **a**, **ship**, **duck**, **sea**, **lee**, **free**, **star**, **lar**, and **gar**, and then extrapolate.

Tack

Based on the large number of collisions at sea, it would appear that no one properly understands any of the many nautical meanings of **tack**, so don't spend too much time on them:

1. Direction of the wind with respect to the centerline of the boat, or possibly vice versa. This is impossible to explain without diagrams (as well as with them).

2. One of the corners of a triangular sail, or one of the corners of a square sail, or a rope attached to it, or possibly vice versa, or not.

3. A kind of biscuit favored by sailors with steel jaws; somewhat less pleasant to eat than the office supply after which it is named. The type of biscuit known as "hardtack" is the only material that can scratch a diamond. The record for swallowing the most hardtack biscuits in a lifetime (seven) is held by Ulysses S.S. Constitution (known as "Old Iron-Insides" to his fellow sailors).

4. (Thaumaturgy) To sail into the wind; to turn so as to sail into the wind; to turn through the wind; an instance of sailing into the wind; an instance of turning so as to sail into the wind; an instance of turning through the wind; several instances of turning through the wind; several instances of

turning so as to sail into a turn sailing through into the sail in the wind to turn sail turn wind sail; etc.; etc.

As an equally ambiguous substitute for this last definition, consider using the word **beat,** which appears in at least one sailing dictionary thus:

beat, a—Tacks, series of, a.

beat, to—Tacks, series of, a, to make.

beating—Tacks, series of, a, making.

Tacking was once thought to be impossible, and ships were typically built for one-way trips only. Those familiar paintings of Columbus's ships running majestically before the wind with their big square sails flying should leave observant viewers wondering: *how did he plan to go back?* The answer, of course—assuming the world did turn out to be flat, which of course it did—is that he relied on outboard motors, bungee cords, trails of bread crumbs, etc. To Columbus's relief, none of these artificial methods ended up being necessary, as the shores of the New World were found to be teeming with friendly dolphins willing to do all the heavy hauling.[66]

> ## GLOSSARY
>
> *harbor pilot*—
> *Valet parking
> service (wet).*

---

66. Ancestors of the original Teemsters.

Tacking, while still barely understood, has at least been shown not to be in violation of any known laws of pressure or suction (thanks in part to the recent and astonishingly fortuitous discovery of the Principle of Sailing Suckage).

Port

How such a short word can have so many unrelated definitions (eight at last count; possibly more by the time you finish reading this sentence) is beyond all human comprehension:

1. Where a boat spends its time when it's not on duty.

2. The left side of the boat, regardless of which side is actually closer to the nearest port.

3. A **porthole** (window), regardless of which side of the boat it's on.[67] Since a porthole is not actually a hole, it is sometimes called a **portlight**, due to the fact that it is not actually a light either.

4. A wine which sailors are not above drinking, if they can just find a quiet place to lay it down and then be patient for twenty years while it ages.

5. To carry (on a boat).

67. That is, you may encounter a "starboard porthole" . . . in the same way that you can encounter a "startable portable" or a "star-filled portfolio" or a "startling Portuguese." There is even such a thing as a "starvation portion"; they serve them at the Portland Starbucks.

GLOSSARY

self-referential
definition—
This.

6. To carry (a boat).

7. To turn (a boat) to port.

8. To lose all meaning by being saddled with too many unrelated definitions.

USAGE QUIZ #4

1. Perform the following computations, showing your work at each step:

   If a third officer can't tell the difference between two half hitches and a figure-eight on a ten-foot foreguy at six bells, this can be blamed on how many fifths of Seagram's Seven? _____

   When will he deep-six the empties? _____

   And how will he make it back to quarters pie-eyed? _____

   _____

2. Do any of the following have anything to do with sailing?

   a. flying_____

   b. hiking _____

   c. running_____

   d. walking_____

   _____

3. . . . as in:

   a. _____ the jib

   b. _____out on the gunwale

   c. _____ aground

   d. _____pneumonia

4. Pronounce any of the following terms out loud without giggling or getting slapped:

    a. clumbungay

    b. thole

    c. pintle

    d. rubber snubber

_____

5. How can you have missed the boat so completely and still find yourself so utterly at sea? _____

    _____

    _____

6. Offshore breezes and offshore oil rigs and offshore bank accounts and offshore fishing are all offshore. What does that imply about their liquidity? _____

    _____

    _____

7. Vote for your favorite non-existent nautical term (one vote per customer, please):

    ☐   a. narrowside

    ☐   b. starboardhole

    ☐   c. underboard

    ☐   d. sober captain

_____

8. Explain (in words of not less than a dozen syllables each) why it is that:
   - ◆ trains go on rails
   - ◆ rails go on ships
   - ◆ train wheels go on trucks
   - ◆ trucks go on ships' masts
   - ◆ training wheels go on trikes
   - ◆ we'll have no truck with those who go on railing against training master shippers

9. Which of these expressions are you least likely to hear while sailing?
   - ☐ a. "Belay yer after taffrail and gudgeon her to windward."
   - ☐ b. " *Ishmael*'? How's about we just call you 'Fruitcake'?"
   - ☐ c. "Man those ships, ship those battens, batten those hatches, hatch those plans, and get all this gooey stuff off my nice spiffy uniform."
   - ☐ d. "He ain't dimmed his brights, I ain't a-dimmin' mine."

10. Become famous for your thoroughly annoying way of interrupting people and asking them why they keep saying "belowdecks" when their boat only has one deck.

11. What *shall* we do with the drunken sailor, earl-aye in the morning?

☐　a.　Put 'im in a longboat 'til 'e's sober.

☐　b.　Heave 'im by the leg in a runnin' bowline.

☐　c.　Fix 'im a double Bloody Mary.

☐　d.　Promote 'im.

HEAD 'EM UP
...move 'em out

Wynken, Blynken, and Nod one night
Sailed off in a wooden shoe—
It sank and they drowned and it serves them right:
Feeble-mindedness and moronism must ever be eradicated
from the gene pools of ascendant populations.
—Eugene Nix,
Three Generations of Imbeciles Are Enough

Now that we know our way around the boat (more or less) (mostly less), it's time to try actually going somewhere in it.[68]

Take this boat and shove it
off

There is an art to starting and stopping a boat. The art of starting is by far the easier; there are only two steps. The first step is to **embargo** (meaning, liter-

---

68. You did know we could do that, didn't you?

ally, "get onto the boat"—often under duress, and often overdressed). The second step is to release the parking brake and shove off.

Usually, only two things can keep a boat from moving: either it is **moored**
somewhere or it is **at anchor**. We now discuss what to do in the face of each
of these eventualities. (What to do in the face of other eventualities—e.g., it is
hung up on a big rock, it is **at the bottom of the ocean**, or it is **parked in
the front yard collecting moss**—is left as an exercise for the reader.) If the
boat is moored (that is, tied to something heavy that isn't likely to be leaving
the harbor anytime soon), your task is to untie the boat from the heavy thing.
If the boat is at anchor, your task is to take the heavy thing with you.

Moorings belong to the harbor, and their numbers are limited. Conse-
quently, a wise skipper never sets sail without making sure he'll have a mooring to come back to—in the same way that a wise mover never picks up a
grand piano without making sure he'll have somewhere to set it down.

Harbors and moorings are normally under the jurisdiction of the **harbormaster**, a person whose other responsibilities (like his mental processes) are
anything but clear. In cities where boats are the chief means of transporta-
tion, the harbormaster may employ an expert to oversee mooring operations
full-time. This custom originated centuries ago with someone known only as
"O fellow, ye Moorer of Venice" and his wife (the drop-dead beautiful but
habitually unkempt "Dusty" Mona).

Moorings congregate in anchorages. An **anchorage** is simply a boat parking lot. The term **road** means, of course, an onshore thoroughfare, but it also refers to an offshore anchorage. In fact, few onshore thoroughfares lead off-shore—but some do. The rest lead to Other Places (e.g., Rome).[69]

The typical boat has at least one **anchor**, with which it is paired by means of a slime-covered rope or a rust-covered chain (depending on personal pref-erence). The anchor's purpose is to prevent the boat from floating aimlessly over all the waters of the earth (since that is the crew's job).[70] On large ships, the rusty anchor chain passes through a **hawsehole**, which originally meant simply a hole for a rusty anchor chain but is now commonly employed as a general term of abuse.[71]

Anchors lead a monotonous existence: their days consist chiefly in being hauled out of the water and then thrown back in. One particular type of anchor is called a **fisherman**, by analogy with the piquant individual whose days consist chiefly in hauling stuff out of the water and then throwing most of it back in.

If the water is not too deep, the anchor will usually stick in the mud (the original stick-in-the-mud) or jam on the rocks.[72] In other places, where either

69. Actually, it is not true that *all* roads lead to Rome. Some lead to Nome. And some lead to Anchorage.
70. Anchors are thus a Good Idea.
71. General terms of abuse can be a Good Idea. Trading them with someone armed with a rusty anchor chain is a Bad Idea, however.
72. For another Good Idea, substitute Scotch for jam.

the anchor chain or the water doesn't quite reach the bottom, a **drogue** or sea anchor is employed. This works like an underwater parachute, slowing the boat without quite holding it in one spot (since any drogue will **drag**, at least a little—and what a drag that can be). In Viking times, a mead-besotted galley slave once accidentally let his sea anchor scrape bottom; it filled with muck, and the next day all the Sagas reported that "Drugged Drudge Drags Drogue; Dregs Dredged."

Raising the anchor so that the ship can begin drifting again is termed **weighing anchor**; during this process, the anchor is said to be **aweigh** (i.e., coming up). The term *aweigh* is only used when what is coming up is an anchor. Different terms are available if what is coming up is lunch.

Driving

Once the anchor is **stowed** (= tossed any old where), and the passengers are seated comfortably (comfortably being of course a relative term in this context), and you have adjusted all lights and mirrors and checked traffic one final time to make sure the coast is clear,[73] you may signal and pull away smoothly from the curb.

At all times it is vital to maintain a clear idea of which way you want the

◆◆◆

73. Although generally speaking, what's happening back there along the coast should be the least of your concerns.

boat to turn, so that you can be prepared when it does the exact opposite. There are three names for the rotation of a ship (or an airplane, or a bus driver, or any other massive object), depending on the axis of rotation:

- **pitch**[74] — One end goes up, the other goes down, and back again.

- **roll**[75] — One *side* goes up, the other goes down. Lather. Rinse. Repeat.

- **yaw**[76] — The ship changes direction (in open defiance of the master's wishes).

Over the years, it has been conclusively shown that no one can do anything about pitching and rolling. Never the type to concede defeat, even in the face of a stunning example of it, seafarers have sunk an inordinate amount of time (and vessels) into refining the art of yawing. In fact, modern sailing maneuvers often appear to the untrained eye (as well as to the trained one) to be nothing more than the result of an obsessive compulsion never to go in the same direction twice.

Broadly speaking, there are three ways a boat can point in relation to the wind: toward it, away from it, or in between it. A boat pointing roughly

---

74. Also a material used to seal cracks in a wooden ship. Hardens on exposure to air.
75. Also a material used to make the sandwiches they sell on the Staten Island Ferry. Hardens on exposure to air.
76. The word *way* written in the wrong direction, appropriately enough.

toward the direction the wind is blowing from is said to be **tacking**; a boat pointing roughly *away* from the direction the wind is blowing from is said to be **running**; and at all points in between the boat is said to be **reaching** (as this author has also been said to be, at more than one point). Actually, the

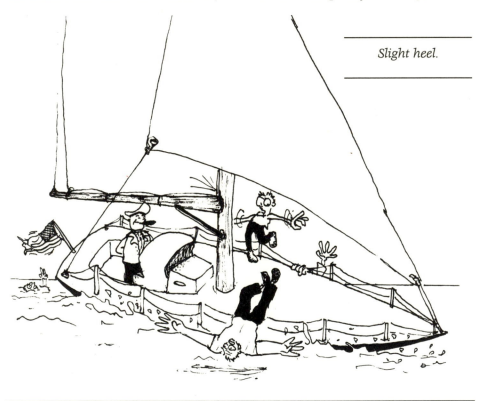

Slight heel.

word **point** is ambiguous: it can take any of the following meanings:

1. To steer a ship in a given direction (in a display of almost touching optimism).

2. Small angular measure (slightly more than a "skosh," but less than a "smidge").

3. Spit of land (avoid with boat if possible).

4. To indicate any of the above by means of the index finger.[77]

Turning more toward the wind is called **heading up**, and in yet another fine display of the imperfect opposites so common in sailing, its opposite is not "heading down" but **heading off** (e.g., into the sunset), a savings of just under two letters. The return on investment is even greater with cumbersome, long, hard-to-memorize words like "toward" and "away from"; sailors prefer to say (in fact—laconic creatures that they are—prefer not to say) that a ship is sailing "into" the wind (tacking) or "before" the wind (running).

Far from being impossible, sailing into the wind turns out to be something boats *like* to do. (For a while. They demonstrate an initial alacrity, but the closer they get to actually sailing directly into the wind, the more hesitant they seem to become about the whole matter.) Sailing very close to the wind is not always wise; this is called **pinching**, and is also one of the less wise

77. N.B. The index finger is the finger *next to* the one normally used for ship-to-ship communications.

◆◆◆

methods of getting a sailor's attention. However, pinching is difficult to avoid (especially on those long, lonely voyages), and certain ships often show a distinct tendency to turn into the wind, or **gripe** (proving that not all the griping need be left to the passengers).

One of the risks of sailing into the wind is a loss of **headway**, or forward motion:

AHAB: Strong current, lad. Best keep an eye on your headway.
REHAB: Er . . . what's my "headway"?
PREFAB: Oh, about fifteen pounds.

In the worst case, the speed drops to zero (or below), and the boat is **in irons**. This expression comes from a popular method of suppressing mutiny, in which the offender is manacled and his uniform is steam-pressed while he is still wearing it.

In desperate times, it may prove necessary to use desperate (non-wind-based) measures of propulsion.[78] There are two main kinds of non-wind propulsion: *Human-Powered* and *Other*. Human-powered propulsion is quieter and more reliable but harder to hide from nosy onlookers, due to the presence of splashing water, muffled curses, and telltale wooden objects flashing violently in the sunlight. These objects are usually **oars** or **pad-**

◆◆◆

78. Pardon the blasphemy.

Purist.

dles, operated by holding the handle (knobbly) end and applying water to the other (business) end. The business end of an oar or paddle is inexplicably called the **blade**; though perhaps not quite so sharp as the blade of a machete, it is at least twice as sharp as a blade of grass, and up to three times as sharp as a jelly roll.

◆◆◆

Man's eternal fascination with drudge work is reflected in the popularity of ships supporting rows and rows of rowers. Synchronized activity is achieved by use of a coxswain, whose only role is to call out, "Stroke! Stroke!" in a rhythmic manner. It turns out, however, that actually *stroking* the oar accomplishes nothing; perhaps a more accurate command would be "Yank! Yank!" (especially if the crew are Americans).

Non-human-powered non-wind-based propulsion is achieved by use of a **motor**, a device for converting dinosaurs into noise. It is rarely difficult to distinguish between a sailboat that is running before the wind and a sailboat whose *motor* is running. For one thing, the motor will be howling louder than the passengers.

Stopping

Stopping is simply the reverse of starting—yes, and aging is simply the reverse of being born. In fact, **stopping** is a kind of putty—used for sealing seams, to be precise.[79]

Intentional stopping is always to be preferred over unintentional (the judges have greater leeway in awarding style points, for one thing). On the other hand, "any port in a storm," as conventional wisdom has it. Often, **running aground** (getting a little too close to the solid part of the ocean)

79. But why on earth would we want to be precise?

◆◆◆

is better than traveling on forever (unless you are a Dutchman and you enjoy flying).

Stopping is easy, as long as you don't talk about it. Once you start trying to discuss what is needed to stop a boat, confusion rears its ugly head (to say nothing of what happens to its ugly rear). A sailor who offers to **bring up** the anchor for your inspection shows a flaw in his upbringing: to *bring up* the anchor actually means to let it down (rather than to bring it up), which can be something of a letdown, especially when you bring it up in conversation. And oddly enough, when your passengers start shouting, "No moor! Please! No moor!" it's precisely the time to think about finding a mooring and tying up the boat—or the passengers.

Once the craft has come to a full and complete stop and the captain has turned off the "Fasten Seatbelt" sign, the passengers are usually invited to **disembark** (the request being phrased in the traditional manner, thus: "Get. Off. NOW"). Slow disembarkers may be incentivized as necessary.

RULES
of the
ROAD

She starts—she moves—she seems to feel
The limpet mines along her keel.
—Henny Wadsworth Youngfellow,
Take My Ship—Please

At any given moment, every boat has a particular course and speed (usually unknown and negative, respectively). For the most part, any proposed changes to either of these quantities are not merely unwelcome but viewed as a curtailment of the rights of the passengers, the crew, the captain, the owner, and perhaps Poseidon himself.

Unfortunately, it has been demonstrated conclusively (often at taxpayer expense) that when two boats both intend to occupy the same spot at the same time, then unless at least one of them changes its course or its speed there is likely to be some amount of disappointment. The rules of the road are mostly a means for deciding which of the two craft should be permitted to maintain its original course and speed. This vessel gets to call itself "stand-on" (although in an earlier, more class-conscious age, it was called "privileged," and damn proud of it, too) and thereafter may use the appropriate abbreviation when signing its name. The other ship is slapped with the insulting appellation "give-way" (formerly "burdened," and goodness knows what some of us would give to be allowed to suffer the burden of privilege).

Penalties for ignoring the rules of the road can range anywhere from a series of dirty looks to instant and permanent submersion. During races, a boat found in violation of the rules is frequently punished with a mandatory time-wasting exercise, such as requiring the helmsman to do "a three-sixty" (turn full circle—generally accompanied by the boat) or perhaps "a seven-twenty" (turn full circle twice) or in extreme cases "a twenty-six fifty-six eighty-seven point two *hike*!" (turn full circle until the boat falls to pieces). Helmsmen seen to be performing one of these penitential acts outside of a race situation are most likely either neurotic or lost (or both).

Proponents of blame sharing and no-fault insurance sometimes argue that in an impending collision situation, *both* vessels should be required to alter course. The only drawback to this proposal is that, like two anthropomorphic rhinos trying to pass each other in a narrow corridor, a pair of stubborn boats could spend the greater part of a day stepping both to one side, then both to the other, in a fruitless and highly annoying mirror dance.

◆◆◆

In fact, the rules of the road would be totally unnecessary if it were somehow possible (as has been attempted several times throughout history) to decide the matter by tossing a coin (preferably buoyant). However, for unknown reasons a complicated and arcane set of rules was developed

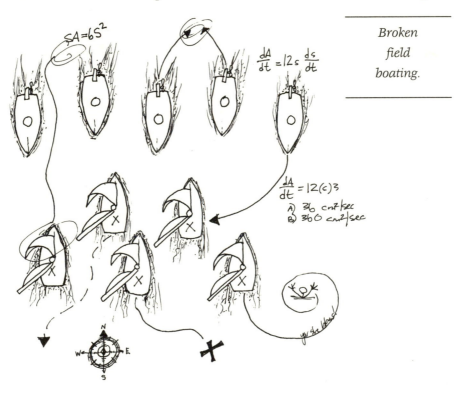

Broken field boating.

instead, armed with which anyone can (theoretically) deduce what any boat in any given situation is expected to do. All that is required is satellite observations of the prevailing conditions, computer projections of each vessel's change in position over time, and about half an hour's consultation with a Ouija board.

Once upon a time, in a simpler day and age, there were obviously kinder, gentler hearts at work—as is evidenced by the fact that the basic rules of the road make a certain amount of charming, indeed naïve sense. So, for instance, the right of way may go to the vessel being overtaken; the leeward[80] vessel; the vessel to starboard; the vessel on the starboard tack; the close-hauled vessel; the less maneuverable vessel; the vessel with the sillier name; the vessel with the pestle; etc. When approaching head-to-head, both vessels should veer to starboard—or both to port, if agreed, but only on alternate Thursdays.

What complicates these essentially straightforward rules is the *priority*

> ## GLOSSARY
>
> ***heave***—*A term commonly found on one side or the other of the word "to":*
>
> ***heave to***—*Pull over.*
>
> ***to heave***—
> *1. To pull.*
> *2. To bounce.*
> *3. To barf (as a result of too much pulling and bouncing).*

80. Pronounced "lured," as in "to its doom."

assigned to each rule under various circumstances. One grim day, someone who apparently had nothing better with which to occupy his mind must have pondered what would happen if a fishing barge running free overtook a close-hauled kayak on a starboard tack backwatering to leeward in a narrow channel on the third Monday in October. Evidently, the question must have been put to committee, because there are now *three* sets of rules—the Racing Rules, the Inland Rules, and the International Rules—each of which goes to some lengths to contradict the other two. The different sets of rules are applied in different situations, which leads to a fair amount of argument when, for example, people are racing over inland waters from one country to another (e.g., to get across a river without being spotted by the border patrol).

A second complication is the rather large number of exceptions to the rules of the road (affectionately called "the exceptions of the road"; unaffectionately called something rather shorter). In a subclause which must surely owe its genesis to members of the legal profession, the rules of the road describe in detail the myriad scenarios *in which they themselves do not apply*. These include the following situations:

◆ **You're clueless.** A skipper uncertain as to whether to stand on (e.g., because it's unclear from his position whether he's risking life and limb or only limb) should give way. "When in doubt, get the hell out," as Dante remarks somewhere or other.

◆ **You're dead wrong.** When a collision is imminent, both vessels must take evasive action. Natural selection helps weed out those who forget this rule.

◆ **The (paradoxical) polite sailor.**[81] In one sense, the stand-on vessel is under a burden of its own: namely, to accept the right of way. Playing "after you—no no, after *you*" is a fine way to foster unhappiness and sow discontent. If either skipper alters his course or speed in such a way as to confuse or terrify the other (not too difficult, considering that he's usually well on his way already), then he deserves whatever appreciative sentiments are screamed at him.

◆ **One of the sailboats isn't.** You may *call* it a sailboat, and you may have bought it at Krazy Kreider's Super House-O'-Sailboats ("We only sell sailboats—no motorboats, no way!"), and you may remember the day the president of the US Olympic Sailing Team ogled it and gasped, "Gosh, Margo—what a swell *sailboat* you've got there!" . . . but if you've somehow managed to get the motor running, it's *not* a sailboat—it's a *motorboat.*

   And sailboats have the right of way over motorboats—

81. As long as we're speaking hypothetically, anything is possible.

◆◆◆

exceeeeept if the motorboat is . . .

◆ **Clumsy.** A commercial vessel with limited maneuverability in a narrow channel has the right of way over everybody,
thanks to the same logic that gives us
the answer to the question: "Where does
a two-ton gorilla sleep?"

> ## GLOSSARY
>
> ***collision course***—*The
> standard method of
> approaching a boat
> which is obviously
> much more expensive
> than yours.*

◆ **Slow.** If—through some bizarre combina-
tion of wind, luck, and voodoo—a sailboat actually gets up enough headway to overtake a motorboat, the motorboat has the right of way. Therefore, upon becoming aware of a sailboat gaining on him, the conscientious
motorboat captain will politely give up his right of way by accelerating
frantically—thus protecting the sailboat from becoming a source of humili-
ation and also giving it a fun little wake to play with.

◆ **Dormant.** A sailboat must yield to a motorboat at anchor (since presum-
ably the motorboat is not likely to change either its course or its speed
anytime soon).

◆ **Dead.** A sailboat must yield to a disabled motorboat. Snickers may be masked politely with the free hand.

The creation and enforcement of the rules of the road have thus done more to reduce the frequency of boating accidents than any other single piece of legislative engineering in the history of navigation. The reason is simple: Everybody is sitting safely at home . . . still trying to make sense of the rules of the road.

◆◆◆

FIRMER
terrors

O Captain! my Captain! our fearful trip is done!
The Minnow's *safely beached for now—and camping's always fun. . . .*
—Willy Whitman,
Skip-PER! Profes-SOR!

One hears a lot about sailors who long to get back to the open ocean (or to some idyllic, uninhabited, miserable little island, which amounts to the same thing). Nevertheless, it is commonly known that when sailors say they're not all that keen on getting back to the **mainland**, they're only posing. Even ships prefer to spend their vacations ashore, thanks to the invention of the **dri-dock** and the **dryveway**, two AAA-approved places where boats can undergo maintenance prevention.

The question is: how to get the boat out of the water. The answer is: it's easy.

Your vessel's assault on the shore will require adoption of a three-step program (which can easily turn into a Twelve-Step Program, because it usually takes about four tries to get it right):

◆◆◆

Landfall.

1. Determine your **offing** (= position at a distance from shore). "Offing someone" is also slang for the action of terminating (with extreme prejudice) an
   undesirable acquaintance; the phony storefronts where such activities are
   carried out have given rise to the opposite of offing: "awning."

2. Select a point of closest approach. This is usually either a **slip** or a **slope**. A *slip* is a man-made, non-slippery surface for dragging a vessel out of the water.[82] Slips are also called **skids** (since nothing can skid on them) or **ways** (as in: "How on earth do you plan to get that big heavy boat into the water?" "We have ways."). A *slope* is a natural inclination (one of the few cases in which it is recommended that sailors follow their natural inclinations); it is also known as the **fore-shore** (yep, no question about it) and is easily distinguished from the rest of the beach due to its tendency to go underwater as soon as enough people have spread out their towels.

> # GLOSSARY
>
> **broadside**—*To turn the ship until its side faces the viewer, so that it may more closely resemble a barn and therefore be harder to hit.*

3. Approach the identified point, taking care to avoid grinding against rocks or getting skewered on a **spit** (a bit of land jutting out into the water; anything bigger than a diving board qualifies).

---

82. Lots of things are slipperier than a slip—most nautical footwear, for instance. In the immoral words of irrepressible comedian Karl Marx: "Skippers of clippers, start shopping for flippers—stop sloppily skipping in slippers on sloops!"

Extraction of the vessel from its element is now a simple matter of hauling. If a trailer is not within reach, it may be necessary to commence **portage**, which is the carrying of a boat by a group of long-suffering people, instead of vice versa. In many ways, this is the safest way to enjoy your sailboat—and after all, it's only fair.

USAGE QUIZ #5

1. Provide an irritatingly smug commentary on the following little proof:
   Given the following precise definitions:

   line = rope

   block = pulley

   tackle = two blocks and a line

   block and tackle = two blocks and a line

   it can be shown (using simple algebra) that:

   tackle = 2 block + 1 line

   block + tackle = 2 block + 1 line

   block + tackle = tackle

   (block + tackle) – tackle = tackle – tackle

   block + (tackle – tackle) = 0

   block = 0

   pulley = block = 0

   pulley = 0

   And therefore: That hard heavy thing that just whacked you on the head—which felt remarkably like a pulley—was nothing.

2. Guess which of the following somebody else doesn't know isn't the proper definition of "boot topping":

☐   a. Stripe of paint along the waterline.

☐   b. Small English municipality in Sussex.

☐   c. Fashion competition engaged in by crewmen suffering from terminal ennui.

☐   d. Garnish for boiled footwear eaten by starving sailors.

3. Put the following in chronological order:

   a. squalling _____

   b. stalling _____

   c. brawling _____

   d. falling _____

   e. bawling_____

4. Explain to an ignorant layman why:

   • the bridge is a room; and

   • the deck is a floor; yet

   • the bridge deck is neither a room floor, nor a floor room, nor a pack of
      cards, nor much of anything else. _____

   _____

   _____

5. Match the following (a to a, etc.):

    a. center of effort   a. point around which a sail is balanced

    b. center of lateral resistance   b. point around which the hull is balanced

    c. center of pressure   c. point around which the pressure is balanced

    d. center of gravity   d. point around which everything is balanced

    e. center of balance   e. point around which everything is gravitied

    f. center of buoyancy   f. point around which something or other is something or othered

    g. center of the universe   g. yacht owner

_____

5. How come there are two Question 5's?

_____

6. Draw an unfortunate parallel between:
*   chafing gear _____
*   foul-weather gear _____
*   second gear _____
*   landing gear _____

_____

7. Emotionally speaking, which nautical letdown would be the easiest to deal with—a cutter that won't cut, a clipper that won't clip, or a schooner that won't schoon?

_____

_____

8. In exactly 500 words (plus hyphens—one smattering permitted), give a compelling argument for or against requiring the condemned man to provide his own plank.

_____

_____

_____

9. How many of the following will never serve any useful purpose whatsoever on a pleasure boat?
   - ☐ a. Rudder.
   - ☐ b. Radar.
   - ☐ c. Rider.
   - ☐ d. Rita.
   - ☐ e. Roto-Rooter.

_____

10. Summarize the most recent USDA recommendations regarding the use of hydrofoil as a waterproof food wrap. _____

_____

_____

_____

11. Choose your favorite nautical pseudonym from the list below and adopt it for all correspondence with the snobs at your local yacht club. Take umbrage at their reactions.

☐ a. Fraulein Windjammer

☐ b. Signorina Regatta

☐ c. Monsieur Barkentine

☐ d. Madame Portage

☐ e. Viscount Frigger-Jigger

☐ f. Mr. Acockbill

Sailor's PHRASEBOOK

What you *hear*	What it *means*
"A hoy!"	"A barge or small coasting ship!"
"Ahoy!"	"Hey, stupid!"
"Ahoy there!"	"No, stupid, not you! *You!*"
"Ahoy there, I say!"	"*You!* Over there! On the barge or small coasting ship!"
"Anchors aweigh."	"Let's blow this popsicle stand."
"Aye."	"Yeah."

◆◆◆

"Aye, aye . . . ."	"Yeah, yeah. . . ."
"Darn that sail!"	"Get some thread and mend that darn sail!"
"Gosh, this is easy!"	[Never heard.]
"Hard-a-port!"	"Turn to starboard!"
"Hard-a-starboard!"	"Turn to port!"
"Hard to follow!"	"How come 'hard-a-starboard' means 'turn to port'?"
"Harr-de-har-har!"	"Just because!"
"Haul away!"	"Pull that for all you're worth!" or (depending on context) "Take that to the dump!"
"Hey, stupid!"	"Hey, stupid!"

"Hit the deck!"	"Get up!" or "Lie down" or "All right, men, let's get out there— and win one for the Skipper!"
"Jackass rig! . . . Dinghy! . . . Ferry! . . ."	"*And* the boat you rode in on!"
"Jibe ho!"	"Duck!" or, more commonly, "Oops! Shoulda ducked!"
"Land ho!"	"I see a hole in the ocean!"
"Ho ho ho!"	"Santa Claus ain't no slave to alphabetical order!"
"Look out below!"[83]	"Oops!"

83. A rather distracting warning, as the lookout is always supposed to be *above*.

"Man overboard!"	"Oops!" or, to be more precise "It has come to pass that a particular individ-ual[84] is technically not exactly on the boat anymore all of a sudden."
"Prepare to jibe."	"The spirits warn of grave danger in your future."
"Protesting!"	"I say, old chap, that was a bit of a liberty you took with the racing rules, what ho?"
"Ready about . . . . Hard-a-lee!"	"Ready for the boat to shift violently? . . . Tough!"
"Red Returning, Green Going"	"On the way back, you'll be embarrassed about how seasick you were on the way out."
"Starboard!"	"I have the right of way!"
"Starrrrrboard!"	"Can't you hear me? I said *I* have the right way!"

84. Possibly the lookout.

"Two whistles!"	"OK! OK! *You* can have the right of way!"
"Wanna start sailing? Then sail away!"	"And the farther the better!"
"Weigh anchor."	"You do the heavy lifting, and I'll do the heavy thinking."
"What ho?"	". . . Could you repeat that last bit? The part just before the scream?"
"You fool! She's acockbill!"	"Hey, stupid! Haven't you learned the *first* thing about sailing?!"

◆

ONE MORE WORD

In general, sailors are a concise lot, and the fewer words you use, the better you'll fit in.

An example of what *not* to say, recently overheard, is:

"LOOK OUT! There's a storm a-comin' our way!"

No sailor would ever waste his breath on so lengthy an utterance. It's inelegant, time-consuming, and highly redundant, as can be seen from the following analysis:

◆

"Look"	This exhortation is virtually meaningless. People are guaranteed to look automatically the moment they hear a raised voice.
"out!"	The only direction anyone *can* look.
"There's a"	Conveys no meaning other than, "I see something you don't see," which presumably was the reason for the utterance in the first place, but as to what the something is, we have no clue as yet.
"storm"	All the essential information is contained in this word; how unfortunate to find it so well buried.
"a-comin'"	Obvious; nobody cares about things that are "a-goin'." Hokey, too.
"our way!"	The only way something *could* be a-comin'.

Thus, our analysis shows that a more authentic way to convey this entire observation is with the following complete paragraph, casually drawled:

"Storm."

DISCLAIMER

The publisher makes no warranty, either express or implied, that this book may be accurate, useful, more exhaustive than exhausting, or worth the paper it was printed on.

This disclaimer is not guaranteed to be legitimate.

about the AUTHOR

Dave Zobel would rather be sailing.

about the ILLUSTRATOR

John Dusenberry has never tried to reason with French toast.